SITUAT

YOUNG ARCHITECTS 7
SITUATING

Foreword by Keller Easterling
Introduction by Anne Rieselbach

Greg Kochanowski
ROEWUarchitecture
Lateral Architecture
Dan Hisel
LinOldhamOffice
Interboro

Princeton Architectural Press, New York
The Architectural League of New York

Published by
Princeton Architectural Press
37 East Seventh Street, New York, NY 10003

For a free catalog of books, call 1.800.722.6657
Visit our web site at www.papress.com.

Editing: Linda Lee
Design: Paul G. Wagner

Special thanks to: Nettie Aljian, Dorothy Ball,
Nicola Bednarek, Janet Behning, Megan Carey,
Becca Casbon, Penny (Yuen Pik) Chu, Russell Fernandez,
Jan Haux, Clare Jacobson, John King, Mark Lamster,
Nancy Eklund Later, Katharine Myers, Lauren Nelson,
Scott Tennent, Jennifer Thompson, Joseph Weston, and
Deb Wood of Princeton Architectural Press
—Kevin C. Lippert, publisher

Library of Congress Cataloging-in-Publication Data

Situating / foreword by Keller Easterling ; introduction
by Anne Rieselbach.
     p.   cm. — (Young architects ; 7)
ISBN 1-56898-573-8 (pbk. : alk. paper)
1. Young Architects Forum—Exhibitions. 2. Architecture—
Awards—United States—Exhibitions. 3. Architecture—
United States—21st century—Designs and
plans—Exhibitions. 4. Young architects—United States—
Exhibitions. 5. Architecture—Environmental aspects—
Exhibitions. I. Architectural League of New York. II. Series.
NA2340.S58 2006
720'.47097309051—dc22
                              2005026345

Contents

The Architectural League of New York

Acknowledgments

Wendy Evans Joseph, President,
The Architectural League of New York

Situating is the Architectural League's twenty-fourth annual Young Architects Forum. Participants are chosen through a competition announced each fall. The theme for the competition, drafted by the League's Young Architects Committee, changes annually to reflect current issues in architectural design and theory. The committee asks prominent members of the design community to serve with committee members on the jury.

The League would like to thank the 2004/5 Young Architects Committee members, Eric Bunge, Ben Checkwitch, and Mike Latham, and competition jurors, Iñaki Abalos, James Carpenter, Keller Easterling, and Calvin Tsao.

Michael Bierut has directed the design of the Young Architects Forum call for entries and announcements for the exhibition and lectures for all twenty-four years of the competition. We are grateful for his time, professional skill, and good humor. Photographer David Sundberg has artfully documented the exhibition. The designers and editors of Princeton Architectural Press have created another beautiful volume in this ongoing series.

The Young Architects Forum relies on contributions from the design community. *Situating* was made possible by the generous support of Artemide, Hunter Douglas Window Fashions, Dornbracht, Knoll, and Tischler und Sohn. The League's programs are also made possible by the New York State Council on the Arts, a state agency. The League gratefully acknowledges the support of the LEF Foundation for this publication.

Foreword

Keller Easterling

Situating is a present participle. It refers not to the noun *site* nor to the verb *situate*. The Architectural League's description of the Young Architects competition qualifies the word. Site does not bracket the issue, they say, but rather points us to a special repertoire of architects as they position themselves in culture. Situating, settled as it is between parts of speech, somehow allows the noun site to be a verb and the verb situate to describe a broader condition or field within which architecture operates.

Most architectural sites are arguably closer to verbs than to nouns or adjectives. Yes, there are particular attributes of a location—attributes that can be given a name, a place, and a clear political role. That pleasure is encountered and teased in some of the work collected in these pages. Still, in these examples, site is not engaged in a way that clings to the sentimentality of place and turf but in a way that simply measures and observes the strange phenomena of local particularities as they mix with other ingredients. The participle situating allows for one of the most powerful attributes of many sites: that they can, perversely, be "no place."

No place might still sadden the heart of the architect eager to provide contextual signals of a particular type of community. Yet with somewhat more alacrity, some architects (these Young Architects included) often find more powerful cultural engines of meaning and community in no place. These sites are no place not because they are mute ciphers broadcasting no signal, but because they are no one place. They travel in distributed fields, in media broadcasts, in scripts of what has been called the "experience economy" and in no-place envelopes like malls, subdivisions, and global spatial products. These are the fabled mechanisms of the tragic spectacle—the ingredients of the ultimate critique of capital, supposedly so perfectly anomic that there is no recourse and no further critique. The absolute stupidity of these spectacular products is meant to cause us to rush to make place, celebrate location, and build meaning where there is none. Yet it is probably a mistake to ignore the naturally occurring stupidity of the spectacle. Moreover, here in the U.S., stupidity is our biggest cash crop, the only thing we produce. It is the great raw material that awaits our creativity. We must use it resourcefully.

And what a massive resource it is. Indeed, some of these Young Architects are understandably excited by the excessive waste, poisoned soil, and dead-mall castoffs of the marketplace. The magnitude of the stupidity as well as its size and capacity to propagate make it at once powerful and top heavy, impenetrable and susceptible to any germ that can be carried within its repetitions. Situating, then, is something like manipulating sites that are targets or distributed components carried and multiplied by the market. To the tragedians of spectacle, it might be pointed out that a public political sphere of culture has not remained frozen in meaninglessness and, indeed, has mimicked the techniques of the spectacle itself. Anything carried along in the market can also be carried along in a public realm that is using the same tools as those found in the market. If one wishes to spread a political persuasion, one uses the "viral marketing" that is used to sell soap—branching networks of messages that multiply in broadcast media and on the web. One creates what the marketers call a "sneeze." A technique of selling can become a technique of political persuasion, or, indeed, a technique of space making.

An architectural sneeze works on a species of site that is repeatable and that is attached to some multiplier. The responses to these sites generate not a single solution but a solution series, variants that are generally directed at the same goals. That means that some of the most egregious and mindless examples of spatial repetition present themselves as an enormous vein of space with an engine that will propagate any new wrinkle that is attached to that space, one that need not be in collusion with its original purpose. So those dead malls, poisoned brownfields, and freight containers look, to the Young Architects, like the seeds of a new idea. They are everywhere, making difficulties for the lovers of place but making good carriers of an alternative contagion. Moreover, they are reminders that, as Marc Augé has written, no place has often been a crucial component of urban chemistry.

Architects are already very well rehearsed in media techniques, but they have largely used these in service of career promotion. However volatile and lively the technique, it has served a more ossified career network that is structured in a hierarchical fashion. Within that network, the Young Architects would only be making their debut in this competition and would then need to wait to be tapped by the brotherhood and promoted by their network.

Just as one sees the habits of space making change to take advantage of multipliers and networks, young architects often find their opportunities in collaborative web networks. Superseding the brotherhood, these powerful networks spread research, gossip, job opportunities, and ideas. Young European Architects (YEA) is one of several such networks operating in the European Union. One fantasizes about the Young American Architects (YAA) and all that they might enjoy from the ramifying effects of association. Most are already finding it more advantageous than the rather sad dream of stardom.

As one who rarely uses the first person and often uses participles of all kinds, I have tried to spread the rumor that young architects are already structuring their careers in this way. As a professor, I have also suggested this direction to the inmates. Since a change in our professional habits seems actually to be happening, perhaps now is an opportune moment to attempt to inflate my association with the idea.

There is no reason why the Young Architects might not use their newfound techniques of media infiltration to sell themselves. Of course, they certainly will do just that. Still, one has the sense that, over the years, there has somehow been an increasingly better fit between the original goals of the League's generation-busting competition and the career goals and habits of the Young Architects themselves. It is clear that they are also fascinated with spreading epidemics of real political consequence in culture and doing so with the very ingredients that have been deployed in forecasting our doom. Perhaps the seduction of careerist self-promotion is rivaled by the seduction of actually being effective—not just in architecture society but also in the larger world.

Introduction

Anne Rieselbach, Program Director,
The Architectural League of New York

The call for entries for the Young Architects competition asked each entrant to explain how his or her work responded to this year's theme, *Situating*. Alongside an edited portfolio of their work, the entrants were urged to consider questions drafted by the League's Young Architects committee addressing just what constitutes a Young Architects site. The questions were framed in light of the observation that architects increasingly share concepts and techniques with other disciplines, creating a more dynamic understanding of site. Entrants were also asked to consider the "siting" of the focus of their work, acknowledging the influence of new materials and fabrication techniques on how an architect defines and addresses design problems. Finally, they were asked to consider how these complexities have necessitated multidisciplinary design teams and what implications and possibilities there are for a practice that situates work within this broad spectrum of identities.

The questions were drafted by this year's Young Architects committee, Eric Bunge, Ben Checkwitch, and Mike Latham, as a means of expanding the League's yearlong program theme, Sitegeist: Nature, Memory, Identity. Speakers during the year were encouraged to explore ideas in architectural theory and practice about site, temporality and indeterminacy, and natural and environmental processes. *Situating* sought ways to demonstrate the ideals and practicalities of young practices within a reframed and dynamic concept of site that equally weights design process and design product—often with open-ended results.

Los Angeles architect Greg Kochanowski transformed his firm STUFF's portfolio into a jigsaw-like series of fabric cushions that could be rearranged in the gallery with the intent of becoming "sites of occupation through the furnishing of multiple territories." With a practice divided between speculative projects and built work, Kochanowski uses the term "VISCO-CITY" to define his studies of "the entropic state of contemporary public space," an environment filled with a heterogeneous collection of material—ecological, cultural, and infrastructural "stuff." His competition entries, including those for an eco-center in Busan, Korea, a campground in Palisades National Park, California, for the National Park Service, and the Fresh Kills Landfill (as lead designer at Roger Sherman Architecture and Urban Design), accommodate growth and change by "replacing the rigid strategies of master planning with the more fluid tactics of scenario building."

Displayed on a field of leaves of varying thickness projecting from horizontal strips, Stephen Roe and Chiafang Wu's installation design called to mind the "open-ended organizations that explore the relationship between material performance and site information" that shapes their firm's designs. ROEWU's work frequently melds information-gathering technology with a project's skin and structure. Their Solar Grass Field consists of hundreds of flexible solar "blades" clamped to rotating cables that are stretched across existing walls to act as a solar collector. The Tallinn Module uses a digitally determined and described structural system to create an irregularly folded module, a basic structural unit crafted from wooden strips, which can be adapted and reconfigured for a series of street furniture. A pavilion, designed for the Athens Olympics, uses a multi-node information feed to activate a kinetic and flexible structure.

Mason White and Lola Sheppard's With-drawing Cabinet, created for the exhibition, held sixty sliding plates that illustrated seven projects, including a paddleboat dock for Memphis, competition entries for an Illinois environmental center, and a Canadian garden. Color-keyed by project, scale, and means of representation, Lateral Architecture's etched transparent plates can be examined individually or viewed as a series of images. Another project on display, Flat-space: Landscape of Capitalism, a case study for reconfiguring the built exurban landscape of Columbus, Ohio, was illustrated by a series of Plexiglas collages. Both multi-layered display systems enact the firm's belief that "architecture and public space are defined more through formatting than form" and so should create "strategies for open patterns of use and interactive temporal conditions."

Dan Hisel's work explores the perception of architectural surfaces and the boundaries of building form. His mirror-clad sauna, whose reflectivity cloaks its presence, is set within a rocky, wooded site. The pavilion's form, only partially revealed by its wood-framed roof and window, allows a limited view inside. Two projects inhabit and redefine preexisting space: The Z-Box, a freestanding cube incorporating storage, a bed, and a dog bed, occupies an open loft space. Like the sauna, its form and function become more apparent when it is lit from within. The Heavy/Light House converts a privately owned, abandoned railway bridge into a small guesthouse. Visitors enter below grade, following a path that, with the exception of a few slots and skylights, mostly masks views of the bridge and surrounding landscape until arrival at an open glass room suspended below the bridge's span—virtually the only exterior evidence of interior habitation.

The 8 Container Farmhouse designed by Tiffany Lin and Mark Oldham of the Boston firm LinOldhamOffice transforms the spatial quality of modular shipping containers. Their linear exhibit display began with an analysis of buildings created from ad hoc appropriations of what has become a contemporary building block: 8' x 9'–6" x 40' shipping containers. The house was designed for a shrimp farm in Dorado, Puerto Rico, where an existing vernacular of recycled shipping containers—used individually or in combination—already served as offices, work sheds, storage, and housing. The architects sought to use the standard module of the shipping container, but their approach, rather than simply stacking or refitting the space of the individual units, erodes their forms to create a more literally open-ended (and open-sided) system, exploiting the inherent modularity of the "blocks" for their proportioning and form-making potential.

Tobias Armborst, Daniel D'Oca, Georgeen Theodore, and Christine Williams, partners of the New York City firm Interboro, strive "to embrace the seeming infinity of conflicting, partial views" of given sites rather than attempt a "totalizing, comprehensive view." With information gathered "on the ground" the design team situates themselves in multiple disciplines—sociology, geography, real-estate finance—and in the perspectives of the sites' multiple occupants to establish an informed means of identifying and representing new uses as a way to create form. This methodology generates a unique design language, combining more traditional architectural forms with cartoonlike graphic narratives, expressed in the exhibition by a two-sided mapped diagram of their projects including winning entries for both the LA Forum for Architecture's Dead Malls and Archplus's Shrinking Cities competitions.

Situating as a means for defining a practice implies a wide-ranging approach to all phases of design. The sheer volume of information available—and a new appreciation for the ambiguity of existing topography, as well as current and potential uses—makes for a different kind of design solution. The graphic intensity of some competition winners' work and installations illustrates the possibilities for complex narrative and design strategies prompted by multiple readings of a given site. Layered narrative and descriptive threads weave together what otherwise might be read as contrasting storylines to create open-ended work that both acknowledges existing conditions and allows for mutability and change over time.

overleaf_*Situating* exhibition at the Urban Center Galleries, May–July 2005
(Photographs © David Sundberg/ESTO)

Biographies

Greg Kochanowski is an architect based in Los Angeles, California. In 1999, he founded STUFF, a design firm dedicated to researching—through both speculative projects and built work—complex adaptive systems involving the material logics of contemporary society. Kochanowski received his Master of Architecture from UCLA (summa cum laude) where he was the AIA Henry Adams Gold Medal winner, an honor bestowed upon the top-ranked student in each graduating class. He has also attended Temple University (BS Arch) and Rice University. Kochanowski is currently a part-time faculty member at Otis College of Art and Design.

ROEWUarchitecture is a New York–based partnership between Chiafang Wu and Stephen Roe. Both received a Master of Advanced Architectural Design from Columbia University. Chiafang Wu received her Bachelor of Architecture from ChungYuan University in Taiwan. Stephen Roe received a Bachelor of Architecture from Trinity College Dublin and a Diploma in Architecture from the Dublin Institute of Technology, Ireland. ROEWU was the 2004–2005 LeFevre Emerging Practitioner Fellows at the Ohio State University. They have been honored in a number of international competitions including First Prize in the Ephemeral Structures Competition, Athens 2003. Their work has been published internationally and exhibited in the U.S., the U.K., France, Greece, Cyprus, and Estonia.

Lateral Architecture was established by Lola Sheppard and Mason White in 2002 from a desire to expand the boundaries of architectural practice laterally, under the influence in art, science, and landscape. Lola Sheppard received her Bachelor of Architecture from McGill University and her Master of Architecture from the Harvard Design School. Mason White received his Bachelor of Architecture from Virginia Tech and his Master of Architecture from the Harvard Design School. In 2003–2004, they held the Lefevre Fellowship for Emerging Practitioners at Ohio State University. Both partners currently teach at the University of Toronto.

Dan Hisel practices in Cambridge, Massachusetts, where he concentrates on contemporary designs that strive to integrate architecture, environment, and bodily experience. His interest in the history and theory of camouflage in architecture has led to extensive academic research and publications on the subject, and he has received numerous honors for his work. Hisel is currently an adjunct faculty member at Roger Williams University in Rhode Island. He received his Bachelor of Architecture degree from University of Kentucky and his Master of Architecture degree from Yale University.

LinOldhamOffice is a collaborative design practice established in 2003 by Tiffany Lin and Mark Oldham. Lin received a Bachelor of Architecture from Cornell University and a Master of Architecture with Distinction from the Harvard Design School. Oldham received a Bachelor of Arts from Dartmouth College and a Master of Architecture with Distinction from the Harvard Design School. LinOldhamOffice's 8 Container Farmhouse was awarded a 2005 Progressive Architecture Citation. Lin and Oldham are both practicing designers for established Boston practices.

Interboro is a New York City–based research and design group. Its subject is the extraordinary complexity of the contemporary city, which it engages through writing, teaching, and professional practice. Focused on exploring the overlap of design, real estate, and ecological urbanism, Interboro has won numerous awards for its innovative projects. Interboro's work has been published and exhibited widely, including features in *Architecture Magazine* and exhibitions at the Municipal Art Society's Urban Center Galleries and the Storefront for Art and Architecture.

Tobias Armborst is an architect and urban designer. He received an Architecture diploma from RWTH Aachen and a Master of Architecture with Distinction in Urban Design from the Harvard Design School. Daniel D'Oca is an urban planner, writer, and curator who received a Master in Urban Planning degree from the Harvard Design School. Georgeen Theodore is a registered architect and urban designer. She received a Bachelor of Architecture from Rice University and a Master of Architecture with Distinction in Urban Design from the Harvard Design School. Christine Williams is an urban planner and writer who received a Master of Urban Planning degree with Distinction from the Harvard Design School.

Greg Kochanowski

The following projects serve as illustrations of my interests in exploring the relationship between architecture and urbanism through the veil of ecology theory. This results in classical notions of design—dealing with ideas of form, space, and permanence—being substituted with entropic conditions of performance, occupation, and fluctuation. The work generates organizations that are transformative and self-organizing in nature, supporting the emergence of other, more spontaneous, forms of occupation by replacing the rigid strategies of master planning with the more fluid tactic of "scenario building." Characterized by mobility and change, these emergent territories affect the spatial, economic, and cultural logics of the built environment by engendering new types of sociability through the deployment and reorganization of material, ecological, cultural, and technological systems.

I practice synthetically, making correlations between discrete disciplines in order to establish new techniques and opportunities for design. Particularly, I am interested in the relationships between rainforests and casinos, prairies and the matte urbanism of Los Angeles, floods and bazaars, whereby the matter of the world is not seen as static and determinant, but rather latent with energy that has the ability to shape the performance of our environments.

re.Park

Fresh Kills Landfill, Staten Island, New York / Competition, Finalist
Lead Designer / Team Leader (with Roger Sherman)

The design approach for Fresh Kills Landfill is conceived to accommodate not only the inevitable ecological changes that accompany a project with such a long life span, but also the political, economic, and cultural ones as well. As such, the park's new name, re.Park, illustrates that change itself is the theme, experience, and lesson of the place.

The first step was to intensify a series of latent "ecologies" from the different regions of the site and then project upon those a series of "transects" (an ecological tool used to monitor the landscape), or schedule of programs—each with its own timeframe—in order to provide for not one, but many possible sets of contingencies and itineraries. The result is that this "new" ground above the landfill cover becomes a programmable surface whose occupants—plants, animals, people—and appearance might change according to the evolving state of the site (i.e. the landfill, tides, etc.), economic conditions, and ideas of leisure and lifestyle. Visitors from all walks of life would have reason to visit the grounds all year round, as the site would neither look nor function the same from year to year, season to season—sometimes even from day to day.

1

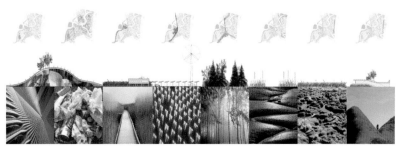

1_ecologies **2**_development of transect network **3**_site plan (twenty years)

2

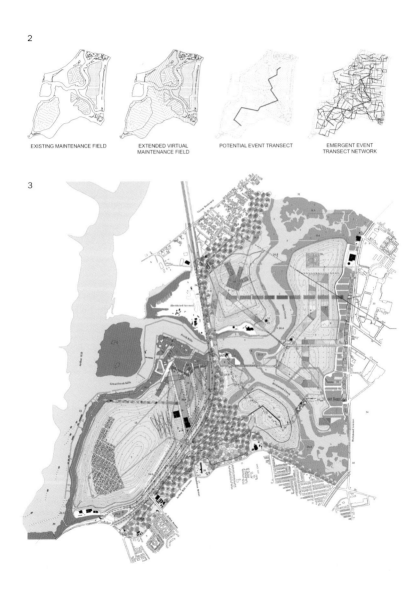

EXISTING MAINTENANCE FIELD

EXTENDED VIRTUAL
MAINTENANCE FIELD

POTENTIAL EVENT TRANSECT

EMERGENT EVENT
TRANSECT NETWORK

3

4

re.PARK Schedule of Upcoming Events		
TRANSECT	**Period Of Use**	**Connection**
01 Flea Market	May–August, Second Weekend Of Each Month, Beginning 2007	
02 Equestrian Trail	May–August, Second Weekend Of Each Month, Beginning 2007	
03 Picnic Area	Annually, Spring/Summer/Fall, Beginning 2007	
04 Sports Courts	Year Round, Beginning 2007	
05 Sports Fields	Year Round, Beginning 2007	
06 Exercise Circuit	Year Round, Beginning 2009	
07 Wet Zone	Annually, June 21 (September 1), Beginning 2010	
08 Landfill Pavilion	Annually, January 1, 2010	
09 Site Gauge	Year Round, Beginning 2010	
10 Extreme Golf	April 17, 2012 (October 10, 2020)	
11 Artist 3 & 4	April 1, 2014 (October 7, 2016)	
12 Campground	Annually, May 15–October 21, Beginning 2013	
13 Artist 2	May 3, 2015 (May 3, 2020)	
14 Corn Maze	August 1 (September 11, 2024)	
15 Playgrounds	August 1 (September 2, 2029)	
16 Artist 1	March 23, 2005 (November 7, 2016)	
17 Garbage Rodeo	August 27–28, 2005	
18 Sculpture Garden	May 1–November 1, 2030	
19 Interpretive Walk	Spring/Summer/Fall, 2018–2024	
20 ATV/ Motocross Course	June 27, 2040 (September 21, 2038)	
21 X-games Championships	September 12–20, 2070	
22 Sky Theater	September 12–20, 2070	
23 Wind Farm	Annually, First Weekend In July	
24 Garden Show	Annually, First Weekend In July	
25 Bocce Ball, Lawn Bowling	Year Round	
26 Experimental Plant Research	Ongoing (Dates Vary)	

5

3 CENTRAL PARKS   =   1 re.PARK

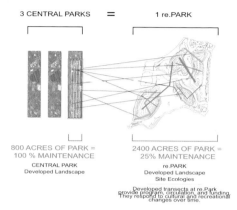

800 ACRES OF PARK = 100 % MAINTENANCE

CENTRAL PARK
Developed Landscape

2400 ACRES OF PARK = 25% MAINTENANCE

re.PARK
Developed Landscape
Site Ecologies

Developed transects at re.Park provide program, circulation, and funding. They respond to cultural and recreational changes over time.

6

NEW YORK SUBWAY SYSTEM
Transit Lines
Transfers
Connections

re.PARK
Landscape Transects
Connections
Destinations
Alternate Itineraries

4_schedule of events **5**_Central Park vs re.Park: generative maintenance **6**_transects as navigation
7_overview of park **8** / **9**_views of model **10**_extreme golf

Railyard Park

Santa Fe, New Mexico / Competition, Finalist
Lead Designer / Team Leader (with Roger Sherman)

In contrast to the historic plaza of downtown Santa Fe, this project treats a thirteen-acre rail-yard site as a living, vital, "working" public place rather than an artifact. It integrates itself into its context by taking advantage of the existing strands of infrastructure that run through the site. The railroad tracks and the proposed storm-water collection and storage network—which not only handles storm water on site but also accommodates the runoff from adjacent urban areas—join together with the linear park, bike trail, and pedestrian paths to form a complex circulation system.

   In contrast to an image of a singular plaza utilized primarily by tourists, the role and visibility of the organizations that front the rail yard are enhanced by a network of smaller, differentiated "yards," each unique in character and suggested use; together they offer a choice of settings for the community of Santa Fe's frequent festivals and events. A mobile system of refurbished, and reprogrammed, railcars are deployed throughout the park and used as "sets" for those yards, which then reorganize both the spatial and programmatic logics of the site. This event-based urbanism is a natural fit with the diverse programmatic makeup of the rail yards and the potential mobility afforded by its rail network.

1   2

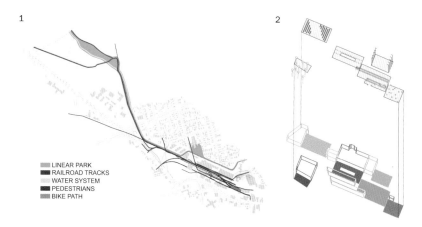

◼ LINEAR PARK
◼ RAILROAD TRACKS
◼ WATER SYSTEM
◼ PEDESTRIANS
◼ BIKE PATH

1_infrastructure context **2**_yard network **3**/**4**_railyard scenarios

3

4

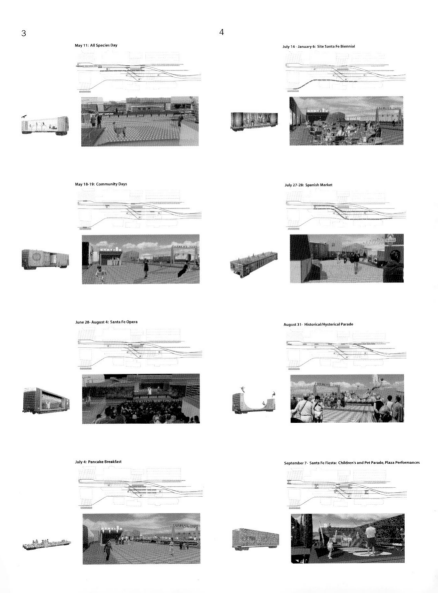

May 11: All Species Day

July 14 - January 6: Site Santa Fe Biennial

May 18-19: Community Days

July 27-28: Spanish Market

June 28- August 4: Santa Fe Opera

August 31- Historical/Hysterical Parade

July 4: Pancake Breakfast

September 7- Santa Fe Fiesta: Children's and Pet Parade, Plaza Performances

Alternate Vista
Marina Del Rey, California
Multi-use Redevelopment Plan / Research

The project, a highly contested housing and film studio development in Playa Vista, provided an opportunity to explore an alternative to both New Urbanist and classical modernist urban development strategies. The site, an abandoned airfield, was divided into a series of plots on which different architects would be commissioned to develop mixed-use housing. These plots, in turn, were governed by a "zoning matrix," which I created, that established possibilities for how each structure could be connected, both internally and externally, to another. This generated a character for the development that was both figure and field simultaneously, oscillating between the individual structures and an emergent mega-interior. I chose to develop one of the individual structures.

Being that the programming of the master plan was focused around the relationship between housing and film studios, I devised a strategy that referenced the public's establishment of identity through the media, such as sitcoms, movies, and advertisements. A prop house—containing furniture, accessories, lighting, artwork, and various building materials—coupled with a continuous ramped surface serves as the primary organization for the project. By selectively choosing the contents of the prop house, this relationship allows users to create a variety of occupational scenarios—from filming to camping—on the ramp, thus generating an environment of constantly changing circulation patterns, adjacencies, and new programmatic morphologies.

In addition to the ramp, the prop house is also adjacent to a series of housing units, also used as film locations or "showcase rooms" when vacant. The contents of the prop house offer an ever-changing flow of material and allow users to customize (decorate) their rooms as they see fit. This establishes a programmatic "feedback system" whereby residences not only serve as locations for filming but also become mechanisms to disseminate particular "lifestyles"— similar to the *Truman Show*. In this, the project proposes that through the deployment of specific material fields and the temporal structuring of particular products/props, a new type of "social condenser" is established—one which itself oscillates through the multiple contingent identities of its inhabitants.

1_programmatic viscosity **2**_hotel vs. movie studio **3**_feedback loops **4**_entropic enablers

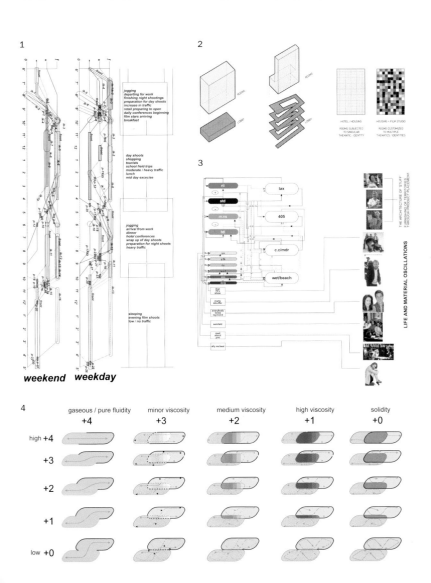

1

jogging
departing for work
finishing night shootings
preparation for day shoots
increase in traffic
retail preparing to open
daily conferences beginning
film stars arriving
breakfast

day shoots
shopping
tourists
school field trips
moderate / heavy traffic
lunch
mid day excercise

jogging
arrival from work
dinner
hotel conferences
wrap up of day shoots
preparation for night shoots
heavy traffic

sleeping
evening film shoots
low / no traffic

weekend weekday

2

HOTEL · HOUSING

HOUSING · FILM STUDIO

ROOMS SUBJECTED
TO SINGULAR
THEMATIC · IDENTITY

ROOMS CUSTOMIZED
TO MULTIPLE
THEMATICS · IDENTITIES

3

rtl

std

m.ma

btl

lax

405

c.c/mdr

wet/beach

THE ARCHITECTURE OF STUFF
FURNISHING OF TERRITORIES &
THROUGH PRODUCT PLACEMENT

LIFE AND MATERIAL OSCILLATIONS

4

	gaseous / pure fluidity +4	minor viscosity +3	medium viscosity +2	high viscosity +1	solidity +0
high +4					
+3					
+2					
+1					
low +0					

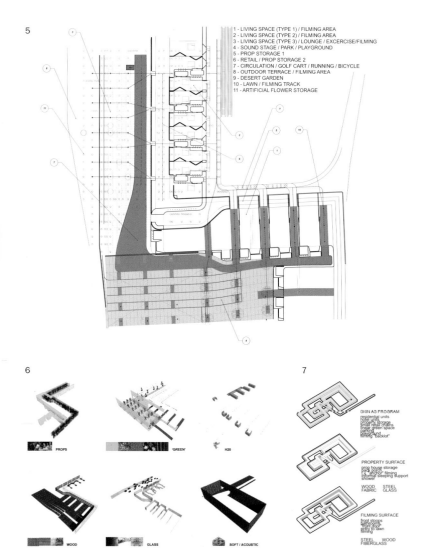

5

1 - LIVING SPACE (TYPE 1) / FILMING AREA
2 - LIVING SPACE (TYPE 2) / FILMING AREA
3 - LIVING SPACE (TYPE 3) / LOUNGE / EXCERCISE/FILMING
4 - SOUND STAGE / PARK / PLAYGROUND
5 - PROP STORAGE 1
6 - RETAIL / PROP STORAGE 2
7 - CIRCULATION / GOLF CART / RUNNING / BICYCLE
8 - OUTDOOR TERRACE / FILMING AREA
9 - DESERT GARDEN
10 - LAWN / FILMING TRACK
11 - ARTIFICIAL FLOWER STORAGE

6

PROPS

'GREEN'

H20

WOOD

GLASS

SOFT / ACOUSTIC

7

SKIN AS PROGRAM
residential units
hotel units
property storage
small retail chains
linear green space
parking
playground
filming "backlot"

PROPERTY SURFACE
prop house storage
park pond
i.e. "hard" filming
informal sleeping support
shower

WOOD   STEEL
FABRIC   GLASS

FILMING SURFACE
front stoops
bathrooms
front door
entry to lawn
filming

STEEL   WOOD
FIBERGLASS

5_enlarged partial plan **6**_material fields **7**_membranes (housing, props, filming) **8**_plans
9_transverse section **10 / 11**_views of model

8

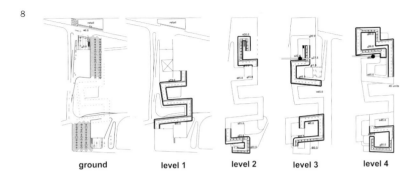

| ground | level 1 | level 2 | level 3 | level 4 |

9

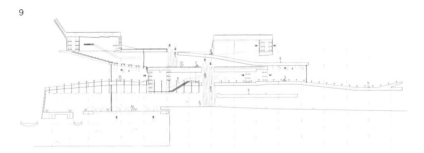

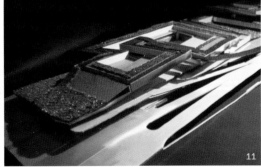

Robbins Elementary School
Trenton, New Jersey / Competition

This project reorients an existing historic building away from its current position as a static, hermetically sealed object toward an open network that is threaded to the community, supportive of various academic and recreational activities, and able to adapt to various changes over time. This is accomplished through a jointly used pedestrian "play-GROUND" around which the school's public amenities— housed within the shell of the existing school—and open spaces are organized. Each amenity is accessed at strategic locations along the "GROUND" in order to allow areas, such as the basement gymnasium, to be seamlessly networked with the outdoors and the public life of the community. Particularly, this reorientation generates new relations, or ecologies, that fuse ideas of academics with economics, recreation with infrastructure, and presents "play" as a generative technique for design.

All of this is achieved by highly programming, if not overly structuring, the GROUND through both material "turfs" and recreational infrastructures. The materiality of the turfs ranges between clay, wood, sand, grass, rubber, Astro-Turf, etc., while the infrastructures include such items as tetherball poles, backboards/hoops, lunch tables, climbing ropes, jungle gyms, and others. By allowing these various systems to overlap and cross-pollinate, the play-GROUND develops a series of flexibilities, in which there is "play" (looseness) between the territorial boundaries of students, faculty, and community that allows reinterpretations of the GROUND to occur. The result is a weaving of the greater fabric of the community-at-large into the life of the school, establishing a nexus of academic and recreational activities.

1_view of play-GROUND **2**_view of school **3**_detail of play-GROUND **4**_new vs. existing
5_program and circulation networks **6**_exploded diagram

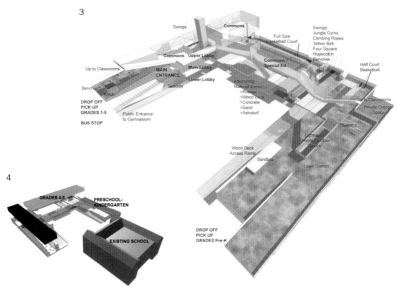

3

Swings Commons

Full Size
Basketball Court

Swings
Jungle Gyms
Climbing Ropes
Tether Ball
Four Square
Hopscotch
Benches

Commons Upper Lobby

Up to Classrooms

MAIN
ENTRANCE Main Lobby

Commons /
Special Ed

Half Court
Basketball

Benches Lower Lobby

Kiosk Security

DROP OFF
PICK UP
GRADES 1-5

Alternating
Material Zones
>Rubber
>Wood Deck
>Concrete
>Sand
>Astroturf

Up to Classrooms

Private Outdoor
Space

BUS STOP

Public Entrance
to Gymnasium

Lightwell
Private Outdoor
Space

Swings

Wood Deck
Access Ramp

Sandbox

Lawn Games

4

GRADES 4-5 PRESCHOOL-
KINDERGARTEN

EXISTING SCHOOL

DROP OFF
PICK UP
GRADES Pre-K

5

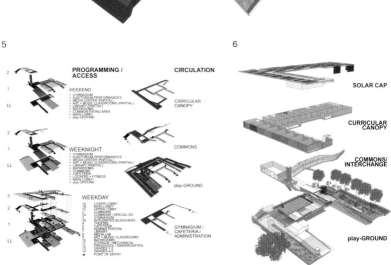

PROGRAMMING /
ACCESS

CIRCULATION

WEEKEND
> GYMNASIUM
> AUDITORIUM PERFORMANCES
> MEDIA CENTRE (PARTIAL)
> ART + MUSIC CLASSROOMS (PARTIAL)
> LIBRARY (PARTIAL)
> BATHROOMS
> COMMONS EATING AREA
> MAIN LOBBY
> play-GROUND

CIRRICULAR
CANOPY

WEEKNIGHT
> GYMNASIUM
> AUDITORIUM PERFORMANCES
> MEDIA CENTRE (PARTIAL)
> ART + MUSIC CLASSROOMS (PARTIAL)
> LIBRARY (PARTIAL)
> BATHROOMS
> COMMONS
> CAFETERIA
> LOCKERS + FITNESS
> MAIN LOBBY
> play-GROUND

COMMONS

play-GROUND

WEEKDAY

1A LOWER LOBBY
1B MAIN LOBBY
1C UPPER LOBBY
2 COMMONS
2A COMMONS / SPECIAL ED
3 GYMNASIUM
3A INTEGRATED BLEACHERS
4 CAFETERIA
5 ADMINISTRATION
6 LIBRARY
7 MEDIA LAB
8 ART + MUSIC CLASSROOMS
9 BATHROOMS
10 STORAGE MECHANICAL
11 PRESCHOOL / KINDERGARTEN
12 GRADES 1-2
13 GRADES L-2
* POINT OF ENTRY

GYMNASIUM /
CAFETERIA /
ADMINISTRATION

6

SOLAR CAP

CURRICULAR
CANOPY

COMMONS/
INTERCHANGE

play-GROUND

Eco-Center at Nakdong River
Busan, Korea / Competition

The project proposes a hybrid institution that functions simultaneously as an extension of the adjacent public landscape and as a private research institution, blurring the boundary between conditions of building, landscape, urbanism, and technology. The center is not defined as an autonomous object or as a building attempting to disguise itself through topographical manipulation but is imagined as a nexus of superimposed and interacting ecological and economic systems that generate new forms of spatial, material, and programmatic interaction.

DEMOSCAPES
The project is divided into four programmatic "scapes," two interior and two exterior, providing a hybridization between public amenity and private research institution. Each is organized to fluctuate between various spatial, material, and occupational states. The middle demoscape, for example, serves as both public recreational space and private research laboratory whereby private corporations utilize the horizontal surface as a testing ground for various sustainable building materials. Access to the exterior scapes remains open throughout the year, creating an extension of the park for public gatherings.

SLEEVES
Since the island is too large for an individual to walk in one day, the Eco-Center serves as a nexus of the various ecologies that comprise it. This is accomplished through a series of "sleeves," or vertical tubes, which intersect the demoscapes. At the base of each of these sleeves is a demonstration and research garden that represents the ecological conditions across the island (plant material, soil, etc.); during the evening hours, their membrane broadcasts research data from these ecologies, replacing natural sunlight with the glow of LEDs. In each case, the physical separations of the island are collapsed.

1

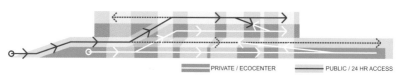

PRIVATE / ECOCENTER   PUBLIC / 24 HR ACCESS

1_8-hour vs. 24-hour access **2**_virtual ecology **3**_plans **4**_sleeves day **5**_sleeves airflow
6_sleeves night **7**_sleeves light

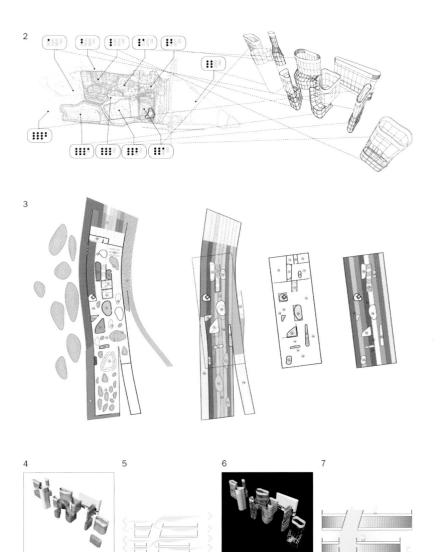

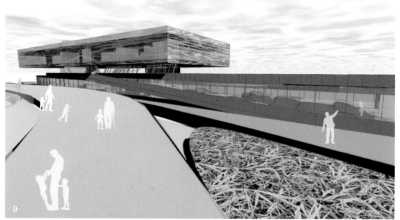

8_aerial view **9**_view from park **10**_site plan **11**_exploded diagram **12**_media mounds
13_section/elevation **14**_view of exhibit space **15**_view from demo garden

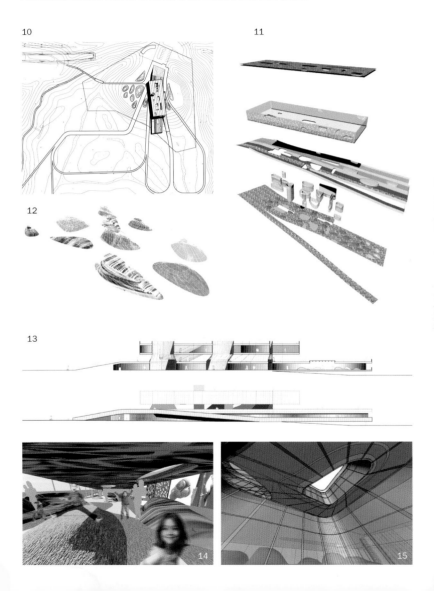

10

11

12

13

14

15

Hut
National Park Service
Palisades National Park, Calfornia / Competition

As a prototypical structure, the Hut is designed to adapt to a variety of geographical conditions it may encounter around the world: from steep terrain, to desert locales, to the preservation of trees on a site. Since some of these sites can only be accessed by helicopter, the Hut is organized into three types of modules, each with its own specific performance characteristics—water collection and storage, general and food storage, and lodging. As a result of advances in manufacturing technologies, a variety of materials and structural systems can be incorporated into each unit, and the geometry of each of these modules can be reconfigured to accommodate the specifics of a particular site.

In addition, the Hut responds ecologically by raising itself above the terrain to minimize any damage to existing ecosystems. This sectional deviation also allows for a variety of occupational scenarios to emerge, from a dense interior during winter months, to an expanded canopy and roof deck during the summer. This multiplicity of uses is not only reflected in the Hut's ability to hold 60 to 110 people at any given time, reducing the need for additional lodging in the immediate area, but also in the manner that it can be programmatically themed—a spa, for example—to connect with various user groups and lifestyle trends.

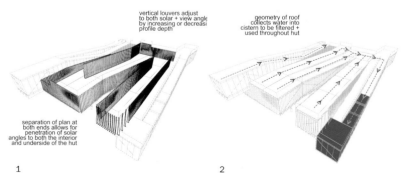

vertical louvers adjust to both solar + view angle by increasing or decreasi profile depth

geometry of roof collects water into cistern to be filtered + used throughout hut

separation of plan at both ends allows for penetration of solar angles to both the interior and underside of the hut

1   2

1_2X louvers **2**_water vs. geometry **3**_system potentials **4**_soft territories **5**_thermal territories

3

SEASONAL EXPANSION / CONTRACTION

WINTER   FALL / SPRING   SUMMER

>PROTECTION FROM COLD
>FOCUS ON INTERIOR TERRITORIES
>CAPACITY AT BASE LEVEL

>HUT ACTS AS CANOPY
>PROTECTION FROM RAIN
>LOWER TERRITORIES ESTABLISHED THROUGH
 CURTAINS + FIREPLACES
>OUTDOOR COMMUNAL MEETINGS / PERFORMANCES
>CAPACITY EXPANDED

>FULL EXPANSION OF TERRITORIES
>UPPER CAMPING + STARGAZING
>PROTECTION FROM SUN
>CAPACITY AT MAXIMUM DENSITY

PROGRAMMATIC AGGREGATION

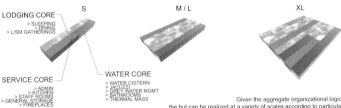

S   M / L   XL

LODGING CORE
> SLEEPING
> DINING
> L/SM GATHERINGS

SERVICE CORE
> ADMIN
> KITCHEN
> STAFF ROOMS
> GENERAL STORAGE
> FIREPLACES

WATER CORE
> WATER CISTERN
> JACUZZI
> GREY WATER MGMT
> BATHROOMS
> THERMAL MASS

Given the aggregate organizational logic,
the hut can be realized at a variety of scales according to particular
sites / situations - ranging from an individual unit, to a megaplex.
This aggregation also allows for programmatic adaptation based
upon regional lifestyle trends.

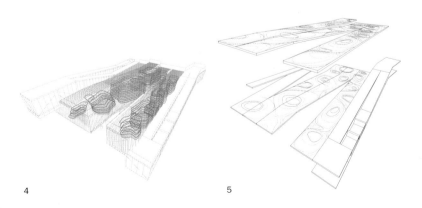

4   5

6

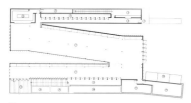

7

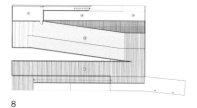

8

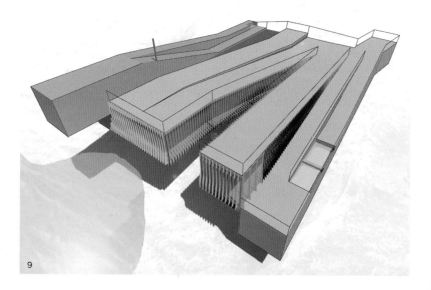

9

6_view of site **7**_main plan **8**_roof plan **9**_aerial view **10**_view of approach **11**_view at roof deck
12_assembling territories **13**_view of dining area

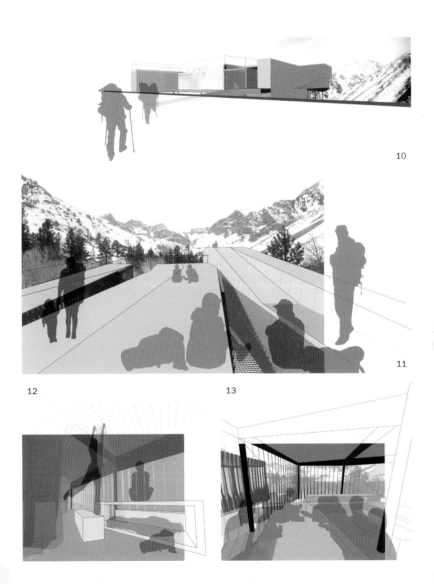

10

11

12

13

Mo(o)re Turf House

Hollywood, California
Renovation and Addition to Single-family Residence
Currently in Design Development, Completion 2006/07

The Mo(o)re Turf House sits as a rotary island within the Hollywood Hills. At one time a larger "camel hump"-shaped lot, the periphery of the site was gradually appropriated by public and private entities that developed an access road and legal easement across the site while the house sat vacant for many years. When the new owner purchased the property, he found himself in a vortex of circulation with no land other than the house. I was asked to provide a renovation and addition to the property within these constraints.

In strategizing solutions, I approached the city to obtain a land swap or other such variances that would allow for the construction of an addition. The city denied all requests but did grant a variance allowing the addition to be built with a zero lot line, on the condition that it still maintain a ten-foot vertical clearance from the street. This, then, became the genesis of the project's formal organization.

Since the property's square footage had been significantly reduced, I established an organization that allowed the client to customize multiple interior and exterior territories through the use of material, thermal, and lighting systems—both natural and artificial—that I deployed throughout the existing house and addition (similar to the casinos in Las Vegas). This created an intensified (thickened) interior network of latent territories that, through their actualization by the owner over time, densify or loosen the house's interior spatial characteristics, change circulation patterns, reorganize adjacencies, and generate new programmatic morphologies.

1_existing house **2**_"after" view **3**_site development **4**_plans **5**_aerial view **6**_exploded diagram
7_library terraces **8**_aerial view

3

ORIGINAL SITE BOUNDARIES

IMPOSITION OF ROAD + EASEMENT
ACROSS PROPERY LINE

NEW ZONING BASED UPON ZERO
LOT LINE + 10FT VERTICAL CLEARANCE

4

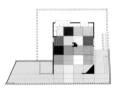 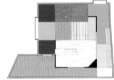 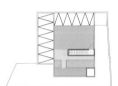

5

6

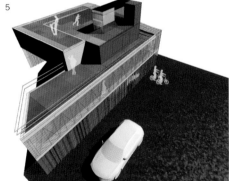

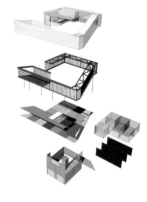
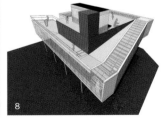

ROEWUarchitecture

INTRODUCTION: MATTER AND MULTIPLICITY
In today's global culture, the question of situating may seem anachronistic.
The specifics of any site are hard to define when infrastructure networks and
information flows are constantly redefining actual site conditions. But it is also
interesting timing to ask this question as the proliferation of information has
generated increasing numbers of situations in which virtual information networks
start to blend with actual reality. Our work goes beyond a conventional operation
of siting in architecture, where the building is treated as an object in its environment. We suggest an open system that adapts and re-creates the environment by
exploiting tangible relationships between an unseen virtual spectrum of intensities and the actual material effects they produce.

Digital design tools allow architects to respond to, and operate with, multiple parameters: computer numerically controlled (CNC) fabrication techniques directly translate these abstract relations from the virtual environment to actual material. Actualization no longer takes place only as a final result of the process or as a representation of that result. Materialization becomes a part of the design process feeding back in a continuous loop with the virtual operations that organize its patterns of deployment. Because physical materials exhibit qualitative variations as a result of their inherent organizational structures, the propensity and tendencies embedded in the materials themselves provide the parameters to calculate and calibrate the performance as a whole.

The work shown here operates on different scales and explores the many implications of various contemporary architectural issues such as informational organizations, newly emergent material properties, bottom-up tectonics, and the multiplication of forces that impact each project. In the House for Two Engineers, and Solar Grass Field, local information, such as the movement of clouds and sun and wind dynamics, is treated as raw material that initiates the materiality of architecture as well as continuously updating the form and performance of the architectural space. The projects Tallinn Module and Network Structure, the latter for the Athens Olympics, develop tectonic solutions that, while based on information exchange, offer material organizations that adapt for varying uses in different urban situations. Actively dealing with complex ecologies of substantial ebb and flow, the project for the Calumet Environmental Center in Chicago posits an architecture where use-patterns (program) as well as form are precisely calibrated to specific local conditions. Immersive Objects and Paper-thin Architecture, two recent research projects, formulate new relationships between iterative local manipulations and overall spatial effects—situating the viewer within a field of parts that accumulates into a whole new situation. Finally, the installation for the Young Architects Forum itself is an open-ended system that consists of images and physical models situated within a field of fifty-two individual plastic leaves. Viewers' interpretations of the projects vary as they move through and interact with the leaves both individually and as a cluster.

Each of these projects explores a different situation by redistributing various intensities on site and by reconfiguring the environment as a result of recognizing the forces that actually generate particular differentiations and variations. While the reality of a situation remains mutable, it is not randomly configured: delicate maneuvers steer multiplicitous systems in specific directions, resulting in internally consistent but open-ended solutions.

Network Structure

Competition

Caught up in a proliferation of constantly developing technologies, architecture is no longer aiming at being solid and everlasting. We are increasingly looking at the possibilities of taking *time* as an inherent factor in the design of buildings—the changes of flow and information over time. This results in an architecture ready to practice the ephemeral: being able to sensitively respond to the environment and react to the users not only by using the devices of an updated technology but also by incorporating it into the design. Originally proposed as a prototype "Ephemeral Structure for the Athens Olympics" in 2004, the project won first prize in the international competition of the same name.

The Network Structure is a network of node-points linked by rigid and semirigid structural members and by information flows. The nodes communicate with each other both physically and electronically. The system functions as a whole made up of individual elements. This structure is an integral part of the global network, a body infiltrated by information. Unlike a conventional static structure in which each joint is isolated from all the others and sized to take the maximum potential load, all the nodes of the networked structure are able to act together, combining efficiencies to distribute loads across multiple nodes: when one node is overloaded those around it respond to spread the load or tense themselves against it. This results in an overall economy of materials through local intelligence. The wood and aluminum structure would be clad with translucent honeycomb composite panels; LED lighting and flat-panel speakers would be incorporated into some of the panels. The panels would be arrayed in a shingle-like manner that allows the panels to slide over each other as the structure deforms, functioning much like a coat of armor that remains firm while allowing flexible movement underneath.

Different programmatic activities are suggested by different gestures of the system: from informal urban info-hub to a dancing platform, performance stage, or a mutable urban furniture landscape. The system is able to adjust, adapting to local conditions and temporal variations.

Design development carried out in association with Ove Arup and Partners, New York, and Arup Research + Development, London.

1_net structure at the Olympic event **2**_the system as urban info-hub

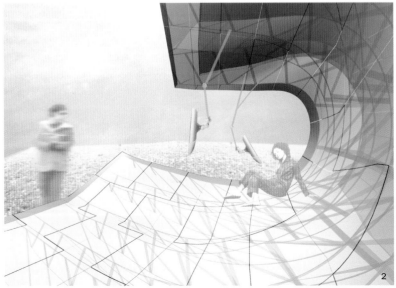

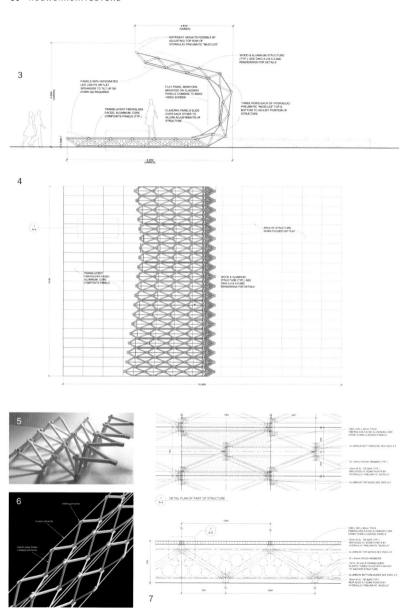

3

4.87M
(VARIES)

DIFFERENT HEIGHTS POSSIBLE BY
ADJUSTING TOP ROW OF
HYDRAULIC/ PNEUMATIC "MUSCLES"

WOOD & ALUMINUM STRUCTURE
(TYP.) SEE DWG A-4 & A-5 AND
RENDERINGS FOR DETAILS

PANELS WITH INTEGRATED
LED LIGHTS OR FLAT
SPEAKERS TO TILT UP OR
DOWN AS REQUIRED

FLAT-PANEL MONITORS
MOUNTED ON CLADDING
PANELS COMBINE TO MAKE
VIDEO SCREEN

THREE ROWS EACH OF HYDRAULIC
PNEUMATIC "MUSCLES" TOP &
BOTTOM TO ADJUST POSITION OF
STRUCTURE

TRANSLUCENT FIBERGLASS
FACED, ALUMINUM CORE
COMPOSITE PANELS (TYP.)

CLADDING PANELS SLIDE
OVER EACH OTHER TO
ALLOW ADJUSTMENTS OF
STRUCTURE

4.20M
(VARIES)

4

1
A-4

AREA OF STRUCTURE
WHEN FOLDED OUT FLAT

TRANSLUCENT
FIBERGLASS FACED
ALUMINUM CORE
COMPOSITE PANELS

WOOD & ALUMINUM
STRUCTURE (TYP.)- SEE
DWG A-4 & A-5 AND
RENDERINGS FOR DETAILS

15.00M

5

6

rotating pin joints

trusque elements

back-to-back timber
v-shaped elements

1
A-4

DETAIL PLAN OF PART OF STRUCTURE

1069 x 500 x 38mm THICK
FIBERGLASS FACED ALUMINUM CORE
HONEYCOMB CLADDING PANELS

ALUMINUM BOTTOM NODE SEE DWG A-5

32 x 64mm WOOD MEMBER (TYP.)

16mm Ø AL. TIE BAR (TYP.)
REPLACED AT SOME POINTS BY
HYDRAULIC/ PNEUMATIC "MUSCLE"

ALUMINUM TOP NODE SEE DWG A-5

1
A-5

1069 x 500 x 38mm THICK
FIBERGLASS FACED ALUMINUM CORE
HONEYCOMB CLADDING PANELS

16mm Ø AL. TIE BAR (TYP.)
REPLACED AT SOME POINTS BY
HYDRAULIC/ PNEUMATIC "MUSCLE"

ALUMINUM TOP NODE SEE DWG A-5

32 x 64mm WOOD MEMBERS

100 & 150 mm Ø TRANSLUCENT
PLASTIC TUBES FILLED WITH WATER
TO ANCHOR STRUCTURE

ALUMINUM BOTTOM NODES SEE DWG A-5

16mm Ø AL. TIE BAR (TYP.)
REPLACED AT SOME POINTS BY
HYDRAULIC/ PNEUMATIC "MUSCLE"

7

3_section of elementary bays **4**_plan with spatial pattern **5**_tectonic and structural studies
6_construction details **7**_tectonic details **8**_different modes of the system **9**_physical model
10_infrastructure-integrated building fabric **11**_overall assembly

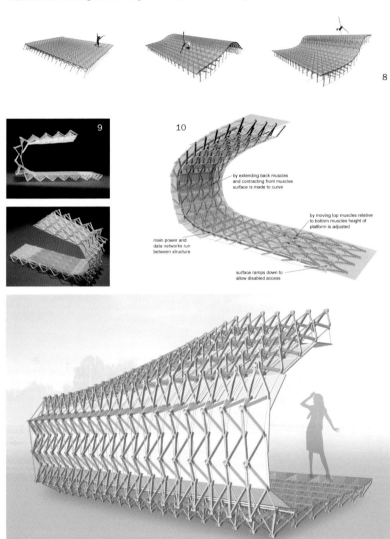

8

9

10

by extending back muscles
and contracting front muscles
surface is made to curve

by moving top muscles relative
to bottom muscles height of
platform is adjusted

main power and
data networks run
between structure

surface ramps down to
allow disabled access

11

Solar Grass Field

Washington, D.C.

Solar Grass Field, initiated from the dynamics of weather and climate, is a proposal for a photovoltaic installation on the blank south-facing concrete wall of the Department of Energy in Washington, D.C. The site is just off the Mall, a location generally dull and devoid of life but traversed by constant variations in weather and atmospheric changes. This local information, such as the intensity of solar energy and wind, became the raw material to transform the site.

By taking phenomenal variations in intensity into account, architecture can be both responsive to its environment and performatively active. We took a field of grass billowing in the wind as our model and investigated the operational aspects of the system: it takes in a constant stream of data from the atmosphere and outputs it through the materiality of the grass blades.

Taking the project as a challenge to rethink photovoltaic technology, rather than applying existing products, led us to a recent development: the flexible PV, a fully functional photovoltaic cell mounted on a very thin, flexible sheet of steel or aluminum that allows it to bend while retaining its power-generation capabilities. By pushing the possibilities of this new material further and making a series of tectonic studies of grass fields, we developed a prototype called the "solar blade"—a component very much like a blade of grass but mounted vertically and capable of generating electricity. Our design takes the form of hundreds of these flexible solar blades attached perpendicular to the surface of the existing wall. The design was developed by starting from the small scale of these blades and working up toward the assembly of the overall system. To support the blades, a dynamic net was set up that acted similarly to the rhizomatic root systems of grass itself.

The effect of the vertical field of solar grass results from a combination of the bending of the blades in the wind, their position toward the sun, and the flexibility of the underlying net. The overall performance emerges from the interaction of climatic information and the materiality of the blades. The result is a vertical solar collector that interacts with the persistent flows of weather to maximize the generation of solar power and to create a constantly changing visual landscape. Solar Grass Field demonstrates the complex, continuous, and entirely unpredictable interaction of building and environment.

1_dynamic net **2**_elevation and plan of the installation **3**_solar blade prototype
4_partial assemblages

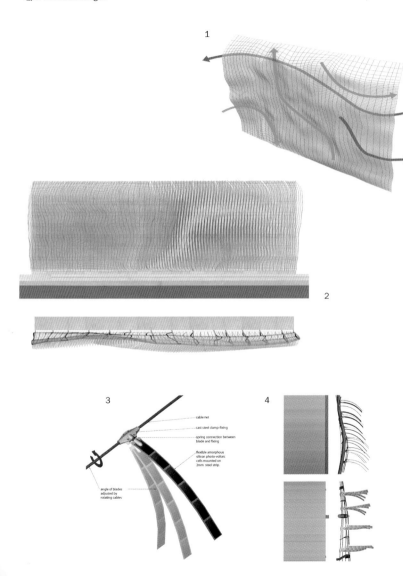

1

2

3

cable net

cast steel clamp-fixing

spring connection between
blade and fixing

flexible amorphous
silicon photo-voltaic
cells mounted on
2mm steel strip.

angle of blades
adjusted by
rotating cables

4

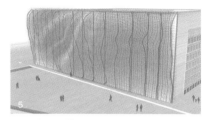

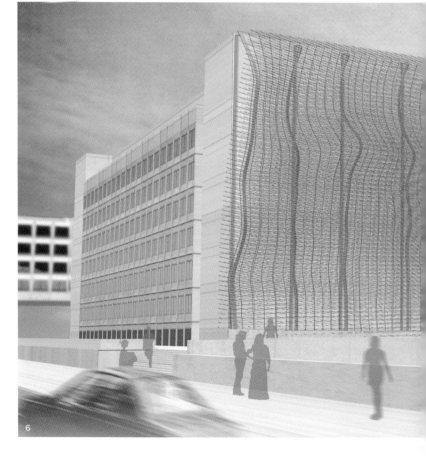

5_aerial view over the solar field and plaza **6**_view from street, approaching the field

Material Life
Design-Research

Examining the emergence of complex patterns and forms in nature, it becomes clear that the infinite diversity of our world is created in part by the interaction of material systems with pervasive differences in climatic and environmental intensities—pulsing, drifting, shifting variations in temperature, pressure, nutrient availability, humidity—from which almost all visible variation in the natural world emerges. Employing this knowledge as part of a design process requires an intimacy between human intervention and the propensities of materials achieved through cumulative adjustments in intensities. Paper-thin Architecture and Immersive Objects, completed as part of a research project at Ohio State University, explore this intimacy in two very different materials: household aluminum flashing and PETG plastic.

PAPER-THIN ARCHITECTURE

Taking paper-thin aluminum flashing, a material with very few structural properties, we explored the possibilities of adding information to the surface to alter the inherent performance of the material—transforming it from a mundane, concealed material into an active, self-organizing structure that generates its own specific spatial result.

A particle field in Maya is a virtual array of points that become vectors of movement—lines—as a result of varying intensities of pressure applied to the field. Applying the array of lines that emerge from this process to actual materials, we studied the resulting deformations and how they introduce new propensities to previously inert materials. Application of the pattern to paper and, subsequently, aluminum revealed a propensity to span, archlike, which can be reinforced by applying lateral force to each end. To fabricate a large-scale spatial prototype from the inherently unstructured and non-self-supporting flashing, we developed a method of "printing" the pattern onto the material by passing it through a large press, like a roll of paper. This "printed" 2–1/2 dimensional pattern introduces structural properties to the formerly inert strip, giving it the ability to stand up and frame a space within the gallery. The nonuniform, though consistent, patterning of the original particle field introduces subtle variations in this performance that give the final result an unpredictable, emergent quality.

1_particle field **2**_folded paper based on the particle field **3**_dynamic objects responding to variations in intensity

IMMERSIVE OBJECTS

Conceived as an exploration of potential new relationships between virtual organizations in the computer, material properties, and their resultant spatial effects, this project proceeded through a constant over and back between the virtual and actual, digital and material, simulations and prototypes. The virtual environment allowed us to play with a system of varying intensities, while material experiments explored both propensities and actual effects. Based on the observed capacities of the material, in this case PETG, we set up a simple fabrication technique to produce a field of unique but consistent modules: the plastic was subjected to a series of variations in intensive pressures, temperature, and gravity—applied for different durations—which produced geometrical diversity leading to various effects. The specific manipulation of each module is based on its position within a pattern that was produced by virtual experiments in the computer. The final surface was made up of 340 individual modules arrayed in an enveloping "fabric." Some of the modules extend far enough to "kiss" another module, producing creases or fold-lines in surface.

The exact form only emerged during the installation; different factors like the distance between the modules and the creases made by the kissed modules all contribute to the final form. The overall experience is one of immersion in a smoothly varying perceptual field, where light, touch, and opticality are all engaged in a constantly changing effect.

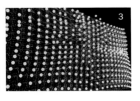

4_test models **5**_printing structure **6**_final installation **7**_surface with different degrees of deformation **8**_intensity study using color **9**_modules combined using nylon ties
10_overall immersive system

Tallinn Module

Tallinn, Estonia

This design of a range of modular street furniture for Tallinn in Estonia combines the newest and the oldest: some of the newest design and fabrication techniques are used to reinterpret and update one of the oldest forms of construction in the world. Estonia is the home of the log building—the very first dwellings made of horizontal logs were built there probably about 2,000 to 3,000 years ago. The log building is based on a tectonic where walls are laid down in layers, accumulating into an overall form—surprisingly like in 3D printing. We exploited this similarity to produce intricate surfaces using relatively simple material and tectonic means appropriate to the local culture.

Folding and twisting a surface can strengthen and stiffen it, but this tends to result in a complex surface that is difficult to fabricate. However, by using straight pieces of wood of uniform section arrayed in a tectonic based on log construction, we can make complex folded surfaces exclusively from one material module, simple square-section wood strips that have been "stitched" together. At a larger scale, the furniture itself is made up of a series of repeating folded modules. All elements of the urban furniture are made from a variation of this basic folded module that is repeated, tilted up or down, extended or shortened as required. In this way, the elements are doubly modular. Because they are all based on the same module, they can be combined together in different programmatic permutations very easily.

Tallinn Module explores one potential aspect of the digitization of traditional building tectonics: By studying the inherent similarities between the iterative, finely tuned techniques of the digital and the aggregative tectonics of assembly implicit in all construction, it is possible to imagine new tectonic solutions. It also demonstrates how the universality of the digital—its ability to represent almost anything—can be applied to generate material solutions with specifically programmatic effect. Bus stop, kiosk, bench, lamppost, advertising column, and even trash cans (along with other hybrid programs) can accommodate multiple user interactions by adjusting the relationship between parts within a consistent tectonic solution.

1_bus stop **2**_bench **3**_advertising column

1

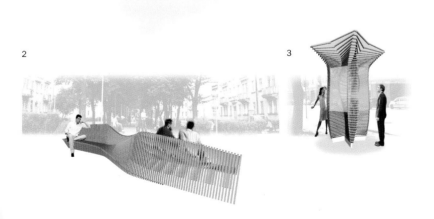

2

3

4

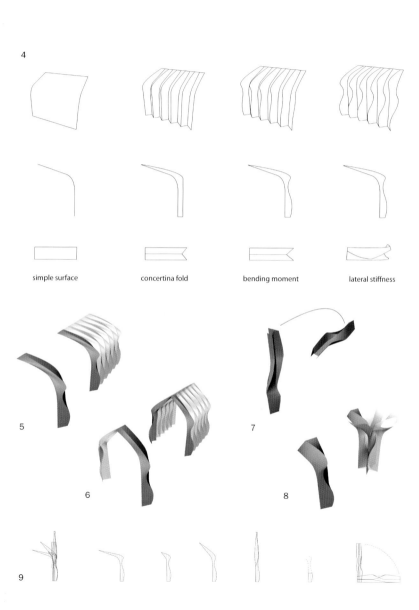

simple surface   concertina fold   bending moment   lateral stiffness

5

6

7

8

9

4_from flat surface to final module—folding for rigidity **5 / 8**_modular components: 5: bus stop, 6: kiosk, 7: bench, 8: advertising column **9**_comparison of modules **10**_plan of kiosk **11**_kiosk

10

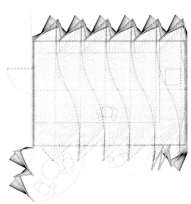

11

House for Two Engineers
Dublin, Ireland

The house for two engineers explores the potential for new material solutions to organize building programs through the production of a range of spatial effects. It uses the simplest of new materials combined with patterns of organization derived from the digital to produce complexity.

The house, located in Dublin, is for two clients who wished to expand their existing living space—despite owning a very restricted lot. To increase the viability of this proposal, we designed a stack of three spaces, each having multiple programs that would vary over the duration of one day. This would be achieved using "the information facade": a curtain wall of intelligent glass made up of two layers of laminated glass with an electrochromic interlayer, which is divided into 2,752 pixels. Each pixel can be individually activated, made transparent or opaque, according to its input. The facade responds to the use of the interior, following three basic modes: automatic—sensors detect when people enter and leave the spaces; preprogrammed—a timetable of programmatic uses for a typical week is inputted; direct user interaction—control panels, located in each space, allow levels of desired privacy, temperature, light level, etc. to be entered. Typical use would involve the interaction of all three of these modes.

Weather introduces an unpredictable element to the performance. Photosensors on the outside of the facade respond to the sometimes-rapid changes in outside light levels. As clouds roll overhead—as they so often do in Ireland—the turbulence of the atmosphere becomes apparent in the facade; it adjusts its transparency in real time to maintain a constant light level inside while providing an ever-changing display on the outside.

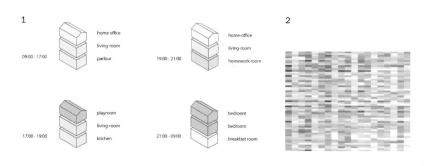

1

09:00 - 17:00	home office / living-room / parlour
19:00 - 21:00	home-office / living-room / homework room
17:00 - 19:00	playroom / living-room / kitchen
21:00 - 09:00	bedroom / bedroom / breakfast room

2

1_programmatic variations over time **2**_an array of pixels **3**_ground-floor plan/first-floor plan/
second-floor plan **4**_interior view **5**_view from street

3

ground floor

first floor

second floor

Climatic Interior

Competition Proposal for the Calumet Environmental Center /
Chicago, Ilinois

The design for a new Environmental Center for the Calumet Wetlands of Chicago,
which is to serve not only as a center for education about the wetlands but also
as an example of the most sustainable building practices, led us to reassess
many of the relationships taken for granted in the design of a building of this
type. We started by developing a catalog of information—programmatic, climatic,
and infrastructural—that shapes and has direct material impact on the form of
the building. We then examined this information for assumptions that could be
reconfigured. For instance, if not all of the building is heated or cooled to high
levels, can this have positive rather than negative effects on people's experience
of the building? Is it possible to minimize the impact of construction on the land
by reducing the enclosed area to an absolute minimum? Can the experience of a
building that maximizes low-tech passive-energy gains teach people about
sustainable development experientially rather than verbally?

Beginning with climatic research and extensive diagrammatic analysis of the
information provided, we grouped the program into two different "climatic zones":
those that require close climate control (sedentary functions) and those that do
not (active functions). The sedentary spaces are enclosed and heavily insulated
to retain heat in winter and to stay cool in summer. By overlaying landscape and
circulation, the active spaces, in contrast, become part of the landscape. A
minimal greenhouse roof covers the active areas to collect solar energy and
protect them from the most inclement weather. Through this analysis, the area of
program to be fully enclosed, heated, cooled, and insulated is reduced by one
third—dramatically reducing energy consumption and construction and maintenance costs.

The environmental information collected and analyzed at the beginning of
the project also directly impacts the form of the building. Its shape optimizes the
flows of light, air, people, water, and energy through it, around it, and over it.
In this way, its morphology makes those virtual flows visible to its visitors;
its disposition and the experience of the space become active teaching tools
in themselves.

1_overall view from main road **2**_building components

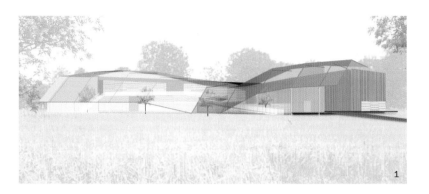

1

2

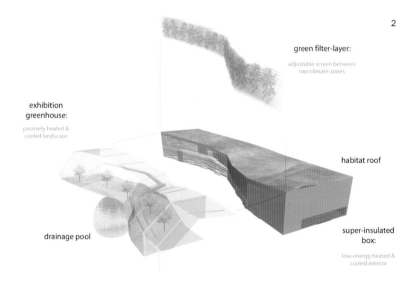

green filter-layer:

adjustable screen between
two climate-zones

exhibition
greenhouse:

passively heated &
cooled landscape

habitat roof

drainage pool

super-insulated
box:

low-energy, heated &
cooled interior

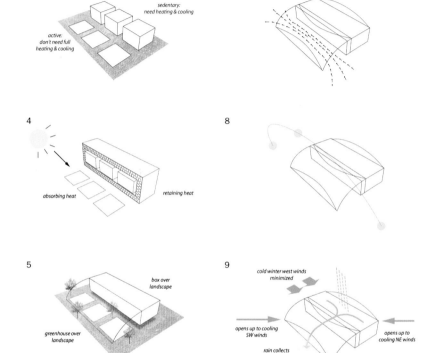

3

active:
don't need full
heating & cooling

sedentary:
need heating & cooling

4

absorbing heat

retaining heat

5

box over
landscape

greenhouse over
landscape

6

green filter
layer

7

8

9

cold winter west winds
minimized

opens up to cooling
SW winds

opens up to
cooling NE winds

rain collects
in pond

10

3_dividing program to minimize energy loads **4**_passive energy saving **5**_touching landscape lightly
6_in-between space **7**_flow of people **8**_form adjustment for sun angles
9_form adjustments for wind and rain **10**_final greenhouse and box **11**_interior view

11

Display Fields

New York, New York

This gallery installation for the Architectural League of New York explored some of the ideas we had already been investigating, now in the challenging context of a gallery display system. The problem was to combine a large number of images of several of our projects, along with some models, to create a coherent impression of the work without imposing a controlling narrative structure. We wanted the audience to generate its own connections—perhaps new unforeseen relationships could emerge—and to potentially create a new experience of the work as a result of its gallery setting.

Our solution was an array of strips that could bend and fold to both accommodate images and support the models. We first explored the idea as a continuous system in the computer. But the need for ease in transport of the images to the gallery was an important consideration; for this reason, the continuous strips were developed into individual plastic leaves that we could use to display both images and models. Using consistent 11 x 17" modules of various thicknesses—some thick enough to project horizontally and support models and others, of thinner material, that droop down and display images on their surfaces—we exploited the variable flexibility of the plastic and its propensity to bend to accommodate the different display requirements. In addition, because the leaves are not attached flat onto a wall, viewing from different angles creates different alignments. The "content" of the display changes with movement past it. Direct interaction is also encouraged: viewers are invited to bend the leaves down for closer study.

Finally, instead of placing an isolated object or image in the gallery space, this display system becomes an intervention in the building: the leaves filter the light within, while from the street, they create a perplexing image that entices visitors to come in.

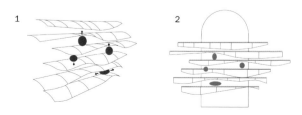

1

2

1_system adapts to accommodate models **2**_horizontal belts spanning over the window
3_view from the street **4**_close-up view in the field **5**_view of the installation

Lateral Architecture

EVERYWHERE AND ANYWHERE

Our design work and research are based on the premise that architecture and public space are defined more through formatting than form. Format promotes ideas of organization and order to inform and influence an experience or cultural condition. Formatting sets up an infrastructure for program, interactivity, and change, and it is in this ordering that site and work merge.

We maintain an interest in the design possibilities of the generic and overlooked. These are sites of everywhere and anywhere—the all too familiar. In these scenarios, design is not about introducing foreign elements, but rather, it is about recalibrating existing elements—whether programmatic, environmental, or physical—through strategies of inversion, amplification, hybridity, and transfer. These strategies reveal what is latent or overlooked in a situation. Architecture is situated in the cultural acts and artifacts of these generic or everyday environments.

The site of our work exists at the intersection of landscape, infrastructure, and urbanism. Through their size and complexity, landscape and infrastructure exist more as field conditions and systems than merely arranged objects. They serve as scenarios for open patterns of use, tactile engagement, and interactive temporal conditions.

The seven projects presented here address either a deliberate specificity of site, the definition of a new site, or the genericness of a nonsite. Where does one site end and another begin? What is the boundary of the situation in which architecture resides? How can we locate a here and there from an everywhere and anywhere?

The following projects offer possibilities for positioning new scenarios relative to the shifting relationships of heres and theres. Negotiating microsites and supersites, our work reformats seemingly familiar situations as a strategy for design.

Recording Memphis

Riverboat Dock and Park / Memphis, Tennessee

The project provides a changing interactive public space for Memphis, drawing upon two salient characteristics of the city: the river and music. The project also serves as a mending or suturing of disconnected site conditions. A large open public space extends Beale Street to the river, while intimate landscaped terraces link the riverfront park with historic cobblestones by embodying traits of both.

The Upper Deck forms a termination to, and extension of, Beale Street. It is a projecting plane that folds and rises up over the river below, providing a unique vantage point and vistas up and down the Mississippi. Within the fold of the deck are a covered waiting area, cafe, shop, and restrooms.

In order to negotiate significant fluctuating water levels, the Lower Dock is conceived as a barge moored to the river's edge, which rises and falls with the changing water levels. The dock provides access to cruise vessels and excursion boats and is also a public space, engaging people with the river's edge and beyond. Recognizing the impact of musical creativity on Memphis, acoustic masts, which acoustically record the changing river levels, punctuate the dock and act as interactive musical instruments. The dock serves as a stage with the masts as its urban-scaled instruments. Each of the twelve hollowed-steel masts is composed of tensioned strings lengthened or shortened depending on the river water level. Notes and pitch variation are created by change in the water level and the height of mast. Visitors activate the strings, causing vibration and sound to resonate from within the mast.

1_model views of upper deck and dock, view from boat approach, and aerial view
2_view from dock **3**_view along ramped terraces

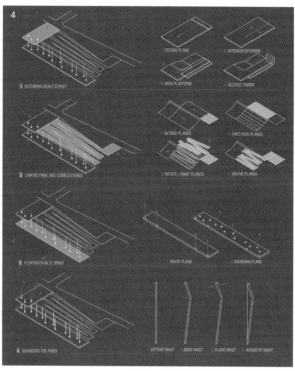

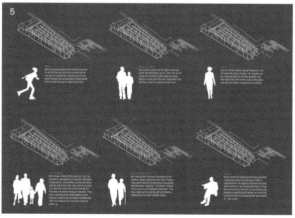

4_concept diagram: four urban elements **5**_narratives: user experiences **6**_section through terraces and dock **7**_section through dock and acoustic mast **8**_plan **9**_view of upper deck

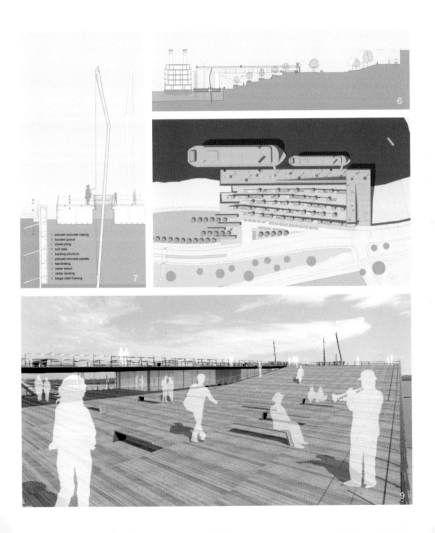

Flatspace: Infrastructural Landscape
Columbus, Ohio

As exurban growth is increasingly consumed by agglomerating retail corridors, its single-use status begins to systemically redefine public space at the margins of cities. This assembly of highways and paved planes is dominated by big boxes and retail power centers, conflating an ever-evolving consumer culture with public space. In this environment, public space as an indeterminate open system has been supplanted by a highly controlled environment of familiar homogeneity. The possibilities of intervening in this exurban condition, what we call "flatspace," on its own terms remains overlooked.

Detached from a larger, complex spatial network, flatspace is comprised of autonomous adjacencies of selfsame components—big box, parking lot, landscape lining. Accessed or linked only by stretches of asphalt within the confines of an automobile, flatspace limits the physical contact of bodies. In its subordination to the car and the ease of mobility, flatspaces are places of sterile transit, or nonplaces. The potential for design in flatspace is less about inserting a foreign program or form and more about positing that the system can recalibrate existing elements and agitate encounters of the public without altering its capitalist dependency on efficiency and geoeconomics.

A typical retail corridor in Columbus, Ohio, served as a case study. Three filters—program, parking, and landscape—are used to test alternate organizational strategies. Each contains three strategies of recalibrated protocols for organization. The nine networks are not intended as design proposals but as strategies or tactics for emergent relationships already at work within exurban corridors.

1_view of Hybrid Pixel scheme **2**_view of Confetti scheme
3_visual glossary of the exurban condition

3

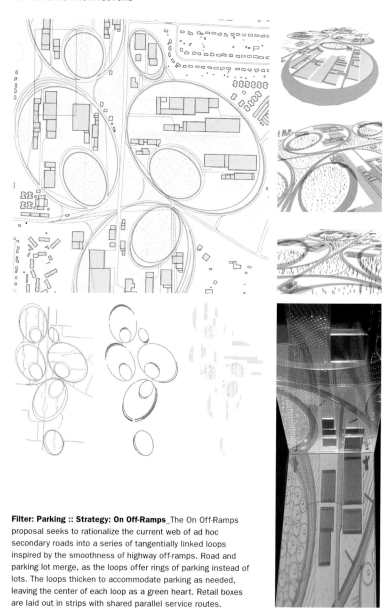

Filter: Parking :: Strategy: On Off-Ramps_The On Off-Ramps proposal seeks to rationalize the current web of ad hoc secondary roads into a series of tangentially linked loops inspired by the smoothness of highway off-ramps. Road and parking lot merge, as the loops offer rings of parking instead of lots. The loops thicken to accommodate parking as needed, leaving the center of each loop as a green heart. Retail boxes are laid out in strips with shared parallel service routes.

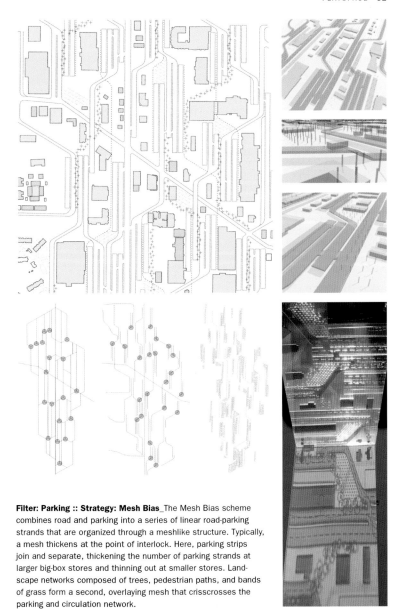

Filter: Parking :: Strategy: Mesh Bias_ The Mesh Bias scheme combines road and parking into a series of linear road-parking strands that are organized through a meshlike structure. Typically, a mesh thickens at the point of interlock. Here, parking strips join and separate, thickening the number of parking strands at larger big-box stores and thinning out at smaller stores. Landscape networks composed of trees, pedestrian paths, and bands of grass form a second, overlaying mesh that crisscrosses the parking and circulation network.

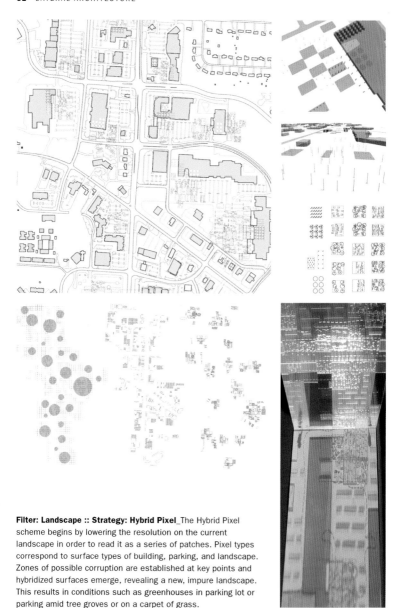

Filter: Landscape :: Strategy: Hybrid Pixel_The Hybrid Pixel
scheme begins by lowering the resolution on the current
landscape in order to read it as a series of patches. Pixel types
correspond to surface types of building, parking, and landscape.
Zones of possible corruption are established at key points and
hybridized surfaces emerge, revealing a new, impure landscape.
This results in conditions such as greenhouses in parking lot or
parking amid tree groves or on a carpet of grass.

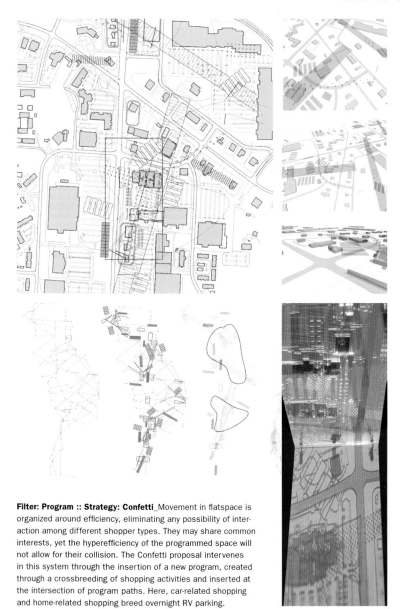

Filter: Program :: Strategy: Confetti_Movement in flatspace is organized around efficiency, eliminating any possibility of inter-action among different shopper types. They may share common interests, yet the hyperefficiency of the programmed space will not allow for their collision. The Confetti proposal intervenes in this system through the insertion of a new program, created through a crossbreeding of shopping activities and inserted at the intersection of program paths. Here, car-related shopping and home-related shopping breed overnight RV parking.

Inside / Out House
Residence / Latham, England

Any residential design raises the question of interiority and privacy. The glass houses of the twentieth century attempted to dissolve visual boundaries between inside and out, denying the presence of services and personal belongings. The intent with this model was to bring the outside in. The Inside/Out House, in contrast, brings the inside out.

Transparent storage walls around the perimeter of the house have a flexible shelving method adjustable to the occupants' needs. Portions of shelves are omitted to grant unhindered views beyond, while other sections of the glazing include lenses for the magnification of selected objects, such as a family photograph. Here, personal items—what makes the house a home—are relegated to a thin walled zone at the perimeter. This serves as a display of belongings, provides a veiled transparency for privacy, and represents a twenty-first-century notion of individualization. No two Inside/Out homes appear alike from within or without, as appearance is dependent on the method of their inhabitation and consumer habits. Your house wears what you own.

On the more private garden side, the glass storage walls thicken to enclose/encompass kitchen and bathroom cores, each bounded by glass water tanks, again revealing operations of the house. An inverted roof serves as a collection point for rainwater into transparent storage.

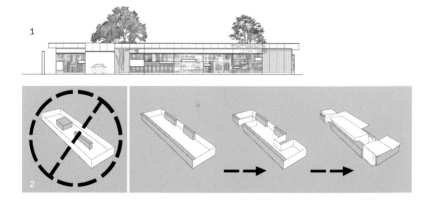

1

2

1_street elevation: storage walls **2**_concept diagram: bringing the inside out
3_perimeter wet walls **4**_customized house for a farmer **5**_view from back garden
6_view of living room with veiled storage walls

3

Between Landscapes
Calumet Environmental Center / Chicago, Ilinois

Only about 5 percent of the land area in the continental United States is composed of wetlands. These transitional zones, neither completely dry nor entirely liquid, are areas caught between ecosystems. Just as wetlands are a hybrid between land and water, our proposal for the Calumet Environmental Center exists between landscape and building.

Each major program element of the center has a "new ground" adjacent to it. Each new ground is composed of a horizontal plane supporting plant life and vertical planes supporting wildlife, becoming a kind of landscaped "room," or courtyard, open to the surrounding landscape. These new grounds are marshes, meadows, prairies—the very ecosystems that make up the Calumet wetlands. The vertical walls serve as nest walls for birds and other wildlife. Here, the building is designed to the measure of nature. The Calumet Environmental Center is a hybrid of landscape and building, adaptable over time as the landscaped rooms overgrow and bleed, performing a gradual exchange between building and nature.

1

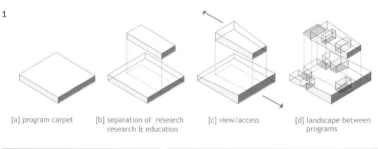

[a] program carpet   [b] separation of research research & education   [c] view/access   [d] landscape between programs

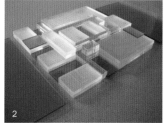

1_concept diagram: massing sequence **2/3**_model views **4**_landscape and program pairings
5_landscape room components

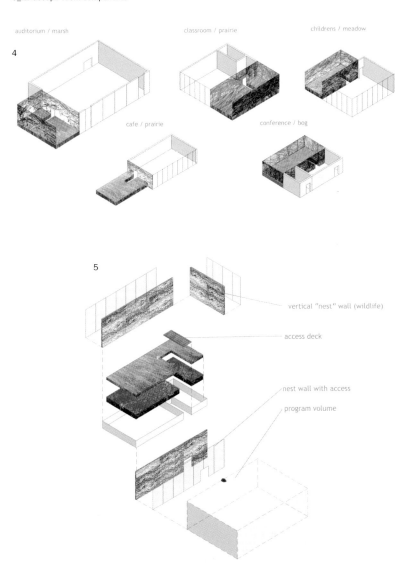

auditorium / marsh

classroom / prairie

childrens / meadow

cafe / prairie

conference / bog

5

vertical "nest" wall (wildlife)

access deck

nest wall with access

program volume

6

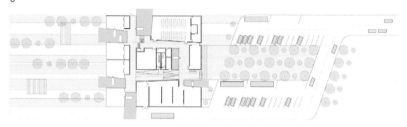

7

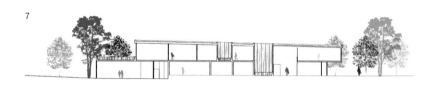

8

6_site plan **7**_section **8**_view of exhibition space with nest wall **9**_south elevation **10**_section
11_exterior view from mesic prairie

9

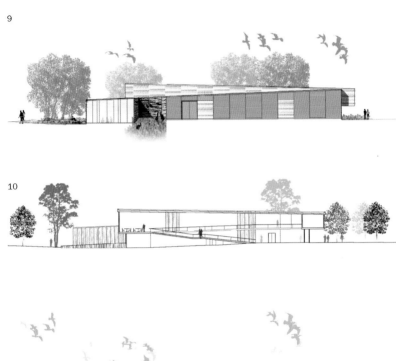

10

11

Soil Horizon

Garden / Metis, Quebec, Canada

The garden is typically presented as an epidermis of green—flowers, plants, hedges—forming an ornamental surface of landscape. Yet a garden or landscape is much more than its surface. There is an unseen thickness, a complex stratification of dirt and soil, that sustains all surface activity. In many ways, there is as much variety below the surface as there is above. The intention of this garden is to expose the thickness of the landscape as a didactic garden of soils.

Samples are cataloged and organized into soil beds with their sections exposed. Each sample has a unique composition of soil horizons. A soil horizon is a layer within a soil profile differentiated by chemical and physical characteristics. Information about each soil is documented on the interior of shipping crates, which remain part of the installation. The garden is part inventory, part scientific curatorship, part map, and part interactive land art.

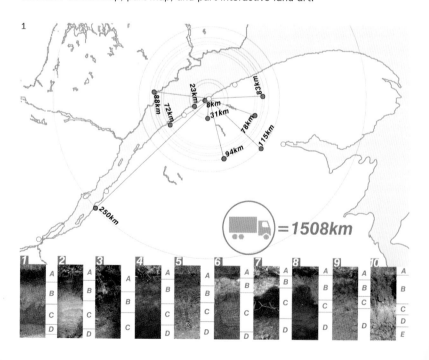

1_map of soil extraction locations in eastern Quebec **2**_soil transport diagram
3_visitor route: the wanderer **4**_visitor route: the scientist **5**_visitor route: the reader
6_organization of soils by soil type and latitude

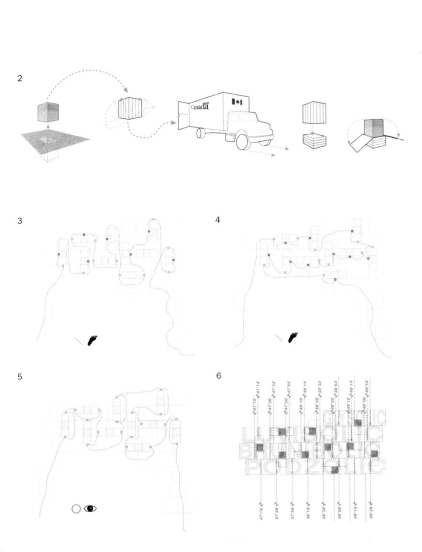

7

8

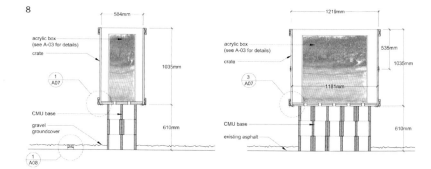

acrylic box
(see A-03 for details)

crate

1
A07

CMU base

gravel
groundcover

1
A08

584mm

1035mm

610mm

acrylic box
(see A-03 for details)

crate

3
A07

CMU base

existing asphalt

1219mm

535mm

1035mm

1181mm

610mm

9

10

7_unfolding of sample from transport to display **8**_detail of soil cube and plywood crate
9_soil garden: crates packed **10**_soil garden: crates unpacked **11/12**_views of garden installation

Migratory Lightfield
Light Installation / Cornell University / Ithaca, New York

In an era of architecture that focuses on the objecthood of constructions, this project addresses design and public space as a field condition, a forum for interactive engagement and effects. The project is centered on a light field, or constellation of light rods, that can be assembled in various configurations. The light field becomes a measuring device of site traits and site dimensions, in this case on the Cornell University campus.

A serial assembly of fifteen plexiglass rods, each composed of eleven segments and separated by semiopaque green plexiglass rings, serves as a filter of light. Each rod is unique, though composed of the same pieces. A xenon light source is placed at the base of the tube; when the light source hits the edge of the rings, it illuminates the color. A field of seemingly hovering light rings creates an alien presence as it rescripts landscape conditions through terrain, structure, and rhythm.

1

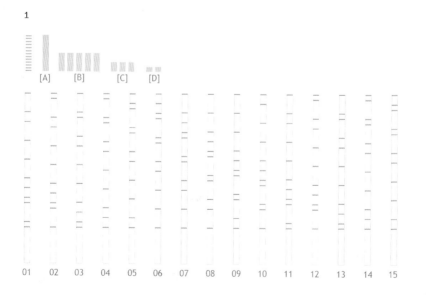

1_light rod types **2**_serialized light rod rings **3 / 4**_bridge installation: rhythm study
5_field installation: herd study

With-drawing Cabinet
New York, New York

The With-drawing Cabinet presents our work much like scientific specimens on glass plates, equalizing the drawings and presenting them as ephemeral yet clinical representations. The cabinet allows the work within it to be constantly reformatted, allowing for new readings, pairings, and patterns to emerge depending on the organization of the work within. Similar to an archiving cabinet, the drawings can be ordered and organized in multiple ways, allowing for new readings of the work.

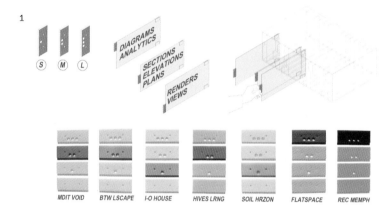

1

(S) (M) (L)

DIAGRAMS ANALYTICS
SECTIONS ELEVATIONS PLANS
RENDERS VIEWS

MDIT VOID BTW LSCAPE I-O HOUSE HIVES LRNG SOIL HRZON FLATSPACE REC MEMPH

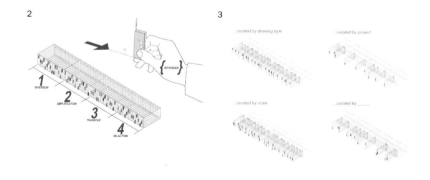

2

1 REVERSION
2 AMPLIFICATION
3 TRANSFER
4 RE-ACTION

{ WITHDRAW }

3

:: curated by drawing type   :: curated by project

:: curated by scale   :: curated by _____

1_curatorial elements **2**_drawing cabinet organization **3**_possible curation **4**_drawing cabinet
5_ghosting of contents **6**_withdrawn transparency

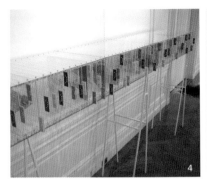

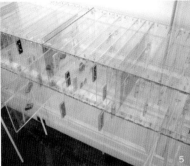

Dan Hisel

The architecture presented here revolves around a question of presence. The research and projects trace several trajectories that seek to understand the vitality of architecture in the world today and our physical relationships to this architecture.

The sequence goes as follows: an early project in the forest (the Cadyville Sauna) that disappears through mirrored reflections inspires historical and theoretical research into architecture and camouflage that in turn generates a desire for architecture that blurs—blurs its own outlines, its own situations (social, historical, experiential), and, by extension, the boundaries of our human distinction from environments, spaces, and architectures of the world.

The second and third projects are concerned less with the optical illusions typically found in the world of camouflage and more with the phenomenological experiences suggested and enabled by tactics of blurring. Through the spatial, sequential, and visual orchestration of the architectural environment, the Z-Box and the Heavy/Light House seek to integrate the bodies of their inhabitants into the world around them. This could be described as a knitting—or a locking together (as in Japanese joinery)—of the individual with its surroundings. My work pursues these ambiguous situations through the extreme integration of environment, space, form, activity, and awareness, engendering a process akin to becoming mottled.

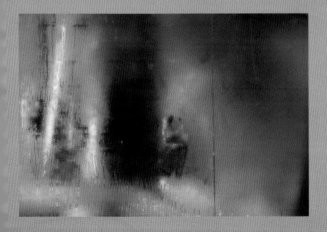

Cadyville Sauna
Cadyville, New York

The Cadyville Sauna was designed and constructed along the Saranac River in upstate New York. It is a compact structure covered with mirrors. It is built up against a cliff; the wall of rock forms one interior wall of the sauna. Twenty feet below the sauna, the river coils into a deep and powerful whirlpool, spinning reflections of sunlight back up on the rocks around it and the sauna above it.

The Cadyville Sauna questions appearances and casts a veil of doubt over the arrangement of all existing structures of the world. Even the natural world is found, through its own reflection on the surface of the sauna, to contain eddies of uncertainty and rivulets of contradiction. What appears to be one thing, one space, one tree, actually turns out to be its double, its inverse, and its representation reduced to the thin silver film of the mirror. Or, one could read it another way: rather than a complicated mirror image, perhaps the structure dissolves, becoming phenomenally nonexistent, and evaporates into the surrounding environment. The sauna's boundary is not simply the surface of glass. This surface, and, by extension the building as a whole, loses itself in the landscape just as the landscape tends to lose itself into the sauna. Either way, the result remains the same: the structure has become "d-y-s-apparent" (both disappearing and nearly dysfunctional), as if the sauna has donned some strange and perfect camouflage.

The exterior slippage of building and nature is repeated (with some significant transformations) on the interior. Within the sauna's intense thermal conditions, surface and form lose much of their traditional meaning. As the heat envelops and penetrates the skin, the body relaxes, heats up, and begins to sweat. The space then actually becomes material: thickening with heat and moisture and the rich smell of cedar, space becomes a palpable substance. In this way, both interior and exterior conditions produce a blur, a fogging, or dissipation of form— a space of overlap between figure and field. Both conditions seen together add up to the following equation: body is to sauna as sauna is to world.

1_exterior view

Where are we to put the limit between the body and the world, since the world is flesh?...That means that my body is made of the same flesh as the world (it is a perceived), and moreover that this flesh of my body is shared by the world, the world reflects it, encroaches upon it and it encroaches upon the world, they are in a relation of transgression or of overlapping...

—Maurice Merleau-Ponty, *The Visible and the Invisible*

2

3

2_exterior view **3**_collage of site showing whirlpool in the Sarnac River and location of sauna
4_exterior view from below

5_exterior detail **6**_exterior detail showing mirror (left) and forest (right) **7**_exterior detail showing door and foundation **8**_exterior view of window **9**_interior showing natural cliff wall with heater **10/11**_interior views

Z-Box

Lynn, Massachusetts

This project is a work of "furnitecture." Bed + shelves + closets + storage + lamp + dog bed = Z-Box, a free-standing cube built inside a large space. The Z-Box solves two problems facing the owners of a newly renovated, wide-open loft: where are we going to sleep? (ZZZ...) and where are we going to put all this stuff? The solution comes through an act of amalgamation: several typically discrete and disconnected pieces of furniture coalesce into a large block of matter. Then it is as if the furniture trapped within this block carefully subtracts the space it needs to perform its work, or accommodate its bodies, resulting in a carved block of perforated steel, polycarbonate, and Douglas Fir.

The ambiguous situation with respect to the identity of the Z-Box (it is simultaneously one thing and several) is further enhanced by the lights within its walls that, with the flick of a switch, transform the box from prismatic steel cube into glowing lantern.

ENTRY

Kit.

1

1_plan **2**_exterior view (photo: Peter Vanderwarker)

2

3

4

3_exterior facade facing living room (photo: Peter Vanderwarker) **4**_exterior facade facing living room (lights off) **5**_detail of metal/polycarbonite skin **6**_exterior facade facing living room (lights on)

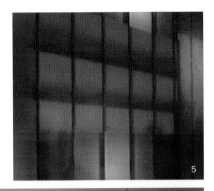

7

7_exterior showing curtains to sleeping area **8**_interior sleeping area (photo: Peter Vanderwarker)
9_view of interior **10**_built-in dog bed for Hank and Lily **11**_recessed shelves facing studio
(photo: Peter Vanderwarker)

Heavy/Light House
Cadyville, New York

PROGRAM

The Heavy/Light House project involves the conversion of a privately owned, abandoned railroad bridge into a guesthouse for one or two travelers. The program calls for a full bathroom, one bed, a small efficiency kitchen, dining area, living room, and deck. The project is 1,000 square feet (not including the roof deck).

SITE

The Cadyville Bridge spans the Saranac River in upstate New York about ten miles west of Plattsburgh. Sheer cliffs of Potsdam sandstone support the bridge seventy-five feet above the deep, rushing water. A hydroelectric power station stands next to the bridge across the river from the client's home. The landscape on both sides of the river is heavily wooded.

The Cadyville Bridge was built as part of the Chateaugay branch of the Delaware and Hudson (D&H) railroad in 1879. This branch was first built to deliver coal and supplies to the state prison at Dannemora and was active for many years carrying timber, iron ore, and supplies, as well as travelers, tourists, and prisoners. The tracks over the Cadyville Bridge were eventually pulled up in 1981.

The client's current house is on property that borders the rail bed, with the bridge at the southwest corner of the property. When the rail line was abandoned, the land was offered to the adjacent landowners. The clients acquired the bridge in the mid-1980s for $24.

DESIGN SOLUTION

The idea of a bridge and the idea of a house are fundamentally antithetical. A bridge is about conveyance—movement along a line, enabling safe passage from one point to another. A house is about coming to rest, stasis, dwelling. To combine bridge with house, to run them together, is to create a collision of principles, a tension between the dynamic and the static, between movement and repose. But the idea of a "guesthouse" spans both of these worlds. A house for a traveler is a place for a person in motion to come to rest.

Inspired by the engineer's diagram of a load-bearing beam, the programmatic elements and activities of this house are understood as "loads" on the bridge, operating in directions perpendicular to the long directional axis of the trestle. While circulation through the house parallels the direction and path of the original tracks, activities such as sleeping, dining, washing, and lounging interrupt this movement, generating spaces and apertures that allow the occupant to contemplate the surrounding environment. Skyboxes, window extrusions, and holes in the floor manifest architecturally these hovering pro- grammatic functions. (For instance, the glass dining table floats between river and sky, pinned in place by views of the horizon.) Thus, these loaded spaces (along with the corresponding sensory perceptions of these spaces) are suspended within the space of the bridge, hovering in stasis, yet extending to the outside world, simultaneously rendered as heavy and light.

Guests enter from the forest through a slot cut into the old railroad berm at the north end of the bridge. This entry, below ground level, precludes any establishing views of the bridge or the river. Initial movement through the house provides only fleeting and awkward glimpses of the exterior world. It is only when guests come to rest at programmatic sites of equilibrium (bath, bed, sink, dining table) that they discover views of the surrounding environment. The Heavy/Light House becomes both light (open to the world) and light (filled with sunlight) at places where the body registers its own weight, where the body comes to rest.

The setting is fully unveiled only at the south end of the house, where beyond a glass wall is an untouched, uninhabitable portion of the bridge. Here, guests can appreciate the bridge in its original condition and gain an understanding of the genesis and character of the structure that suspends them. From this point, they can then either descend into to the glass-walled living room or ascend to the roof deck.

After the compression inside the bridge, the living room provides partial release, as the transparent glass allows the expansive cliffs of surrounding sandstone to serve as the room's true limits. On the platform of the roof deck, everything opens to wind and sky and views extend to the horizon.

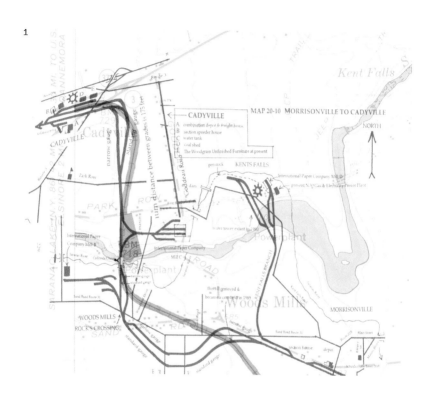

1

CADYVILLE

A combination depot & freight house
B section speeder house
C water tank
D coal shed
E The Woodgrain Unfinished Furniture at present

MAP 20-10 MORRISONVILLE TO CADYVILLE

NORTH

2

3

1_USGS map of vicinity with trestle (shown yellow) and client's property (shown orange)
2_view of bridge from river bank **3**_existing bridge interior **4**_exterior views

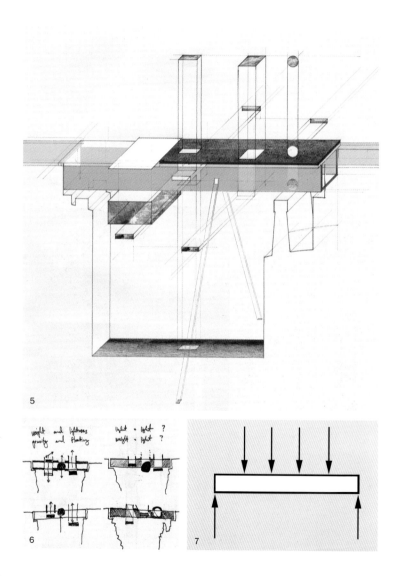

5

6

7

5_conceptual diagrams **6**_conceptual diagram **7**_engineer's diagram of a load-bearing beam
8_exterior view

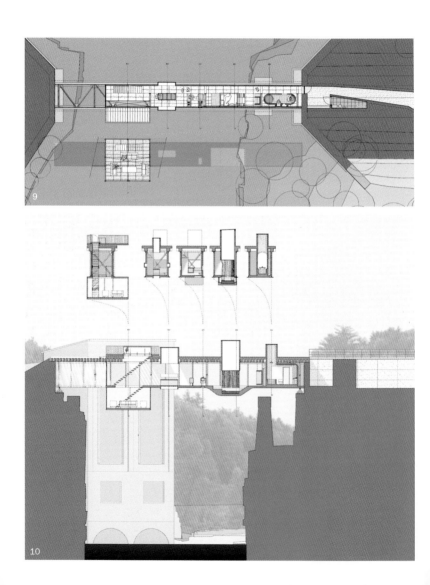

9_plan **10**_sections **11**_view of entry

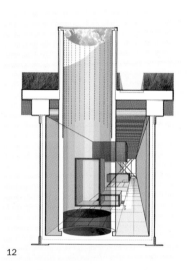

12

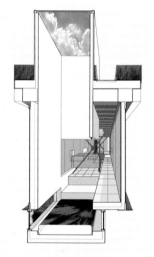

13

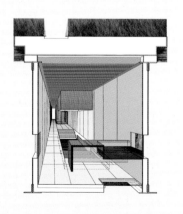

14

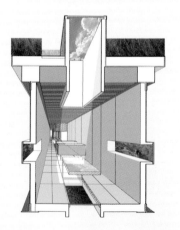

15

12_section/perspective: bath **13**_section/perspective: bed **14**_section/perspective: kitchen sink
15_section/perspective: dining table **16**_section/perspective: living room

16

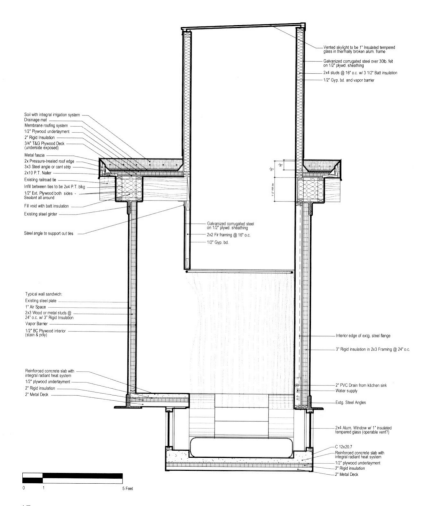

Vented skylight to be 1" Insulated tempered glass in thermally broken alum. frame

Galvanized corrugated steel over 30lb. felt on 1/2" plywd. sheathing

2x4 studs @ 16" o.c. w/ 3 1/2" Batt insulation

1/2" Gyp. bd. and vapor barrier

Soil with integral irrigation system
Drainage mat
Membrane roofing system
1/2" Plywood underlayment
2" Rigid Insulation
3/4" T&G Plywood Deck (underside exposed)

Metal fascia
2x Pressure-treated roof edge
3x3 Steel angle or cant strip
2x10 P.T. Nailer
Existing railroad tie
Infill between ties to be 2x4 P.T. blkg
1/2" Ext. Plywood both sides - Sealant all around
Fill void with batt insulation
Existing steel girder

Steel angle to support cut ties

Galvanized corrugated steel on 1/2" plywd. sheathing

2x2 Fir framing @ 16" o.c.

1/2" Gyp. bd.

Typical wall sandwich:
Existing steel plate
1" Air Space
2x3 Wood or metal studs @ 24" o.c. w/ 3" Rigid Insulation
Vapor Barrier
1/2" BC Plywood interior (stain & poly)

Interior edge of extg. steel flange

3" Rigid insulation in 2x3 Framing @ 24" o.c.

Reinforced concrete slab with integral radiant heat system
1/2" plywood underlayment
2" Rigid insulation
2" Metal Deck

2" PVC Drain from kitchen sink
Water supply

Extg. Steel Angles

2x4 Alum. Window w/ 1" insulated tempered glass (operable vent?)

C 12x20.7
Reinforced concrete slab with integral radiant heat system
1/2" plywood underlayment
2" Rigid insulation
2" Metal Deck

0   1   5 Feet

17

17_construction detail: section through bed **18/19**_computer model: views of interior

LinOldhamOffice

Particularly applicable to this year's theme, *Situating*, the following projects demonstrate LOO's belief that the given conditions of a site are not defined merely by the physical environment presented by a context, but equally as a socioeconomic construct, a legislative milieu, and an inimitable spacio-temporal phenomenon that is independent of architectural discourse.

For example, the first and most elaborated of these projects, the 8 Container Farmhouse, is an explicit response to a number of given conditions. Though consciously embracing the provocative rhetoric associated with adaptive reuse, LOO did not perceive their role in the project as predicated upon a prescriptive manifesto regarding container architecture. Instead, it was motivated by the desire to elucidate the discoveries of an existing local vernacular while refining an existing catalog of compromised forms and spaces. Documentation and analysis of this vernacular led to the design of a house that economizes material means, refrains from grandeur, and is grounded in the concrete realities of its unique place.

LOO believes in the authenticity of site and the inspired potential latent within each situation. Through the more ordinary activities engendered by attempts to respond to a particular problem, the following architectural proposals speak to a common process and a common sensibility: the desire to compose a view, to choreograph a movement, to juxtapose the tactility of one material with the immateriality of another.

These projects range widely in scale and context, from a rural vernacular house to an urban market extension. Still, there is a consistent thread linking each intervention and proposal that evokes our understanding of situating. The point of departure for each project is the same: to first nonhierarchically analyze the specific problem and educe the given potential of each site. Though the method is largely analytical, the intent is to amplify the ephemeral by products inherent within this logical process.

8 Container Farmhouse
Dorado, Puerto Rico

Vernacular responses care not for image, intellectualization, or provocation.
They are engendered through real problems and manifested in viable solutions
to those problems.

The 8 Container Farmhouse is a project for a single-family house located on a
300-acre, 42-pond shrimp farm. Developed on government-leased land, the farm
is subject to zoning laws precluding the construction of "permanent" structures
and foundations. In the 1980s, a vernacular precedent had been newly established on the farm, with the appropriation of shipping containers to provide all of
the farm's architectural needs—from office space to work sheds to storage
space to, most unusually, housing. The farm's existing building history, though at
times spatially and performatively compromised, has nevertheless verified the
feasibility of the basic shipping container as a unit for living.

The 8 Container Farmhouse seeks to expound upon this neovernacular in a
similar way by developing architecture that is conscious of its formal constraints
while embracing of its perceived context. The economic, regulatory, and environmental contexts of the farm provided a clear mandate to continue with the
building typology of recycled reefer containers for the new farmhouse. However,
doing this necessitated a thorough documentation and analysis of the existing
container structures. Cataloging the formal and spatial operations inherent to the
existing vernacular provided a point of departure for the farmhouse design.

The farmhouse design seeks to sustain the lessons learned from the existing
structures while providing a more architecturally coherent interpretation of the
established vernacular. The site strategy locates the new farmhouse assembly as
an extension to and culmination of the series of existing housing units. Maintain-
ing the fifty-six-inch elevational datum situates the level of occupancy at pond
level while providing for local mechanical, electrical, and plumbing infrastructures
below. The central "hinge" container aligns with the established row of existing
housing units and connects the primary programmatic farmhouse blocks around
a central courtyard, a private garden, and four intimate exterior spaces.

Using the eight containers and a series of simple wood decks, the plan
composition carefully choreographs five principal spatial extensions within the
courtyard, toward the existing houses, and overlooking the farm's pondscape.
Each successive spatial extension grounds the occupants in their surroundings

1_site plan of farm **2**_panoramic view of farm landscape

while belying the intrinsic spatial limitations of the 8' x 8' x 40' modules that are used. An existing container on the site's perimeter serves as a storage shed while acting as a spatial boundary and privacy buffer for the neighboring units.

As conceptually provocative as the "container for living" rhetoric may be, the individual container remains efficient but compromised. The vernacular demonstrates the occupants' desires to push, annex, and extend the basic module, since the unaltered unit is not spatially viable. The 8 Container Farmhouse stands as an architectural development of the existing use of shipping containers as a building block for living space. Although forced to adopt the container on logistical, practical, and economic grounds, the design aims to transform the base unit into an operative module for galvanizing a given site and program.

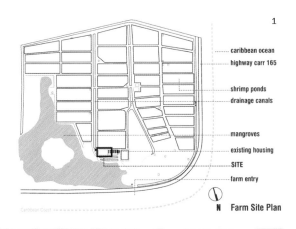

1

caribbean ocean
highway carr 165

shrimp ponds
drainage canals

mangroves
existing housing
SITE
farm entry

N Farm Site Plan

2

ANALYSIS 3_farm components: electricity, aerator, pond, feed, shrimp
4_unmodified unit: exploded axon of one base container

3

4

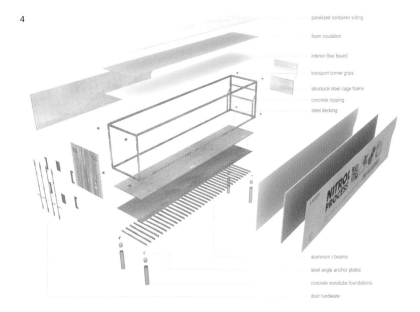

panelized container siding

foam insulation

interior fiber board

transport corner grips

structural steel cage frame

concrete topping

steel decking

aluminum I-beams

steel angle anchor plates

concrete sonotube foundations

door hardware

ANALYSIS 5: Object_Elevated fifty-six inches above the ground on concrete piles, the procession of existing housing units is silhouetted against the sky, appearing as a series of sculptural objects overlooking the pond landscape. The new datum of occupancy serves to negotiate the sectional relationship between a farmscape of excavated ponds and the distant mountains beyond. **6: Frame_** The linearity of the container module naturally directs views and frames the landscape. When arranged in proximity to one another, as with the housing units, the containers inherently compose and construct near and distant views of the farm. The potential for choreographing an explicit perceptual sequence that reveals the farm context became a key motivation in configuring the container farmhouse. **7: Housing_**The typical housing units consist of two containers joined by a wood porch. Connecting individual units appropriates the near and distant landscapes into a shared private realm. **8: Office_** The office consists of four containers joined side by side with a wooden entry canopy. Aligning and adjoining units creates a greater spatial volume while allowing for greater tolerances in construction.

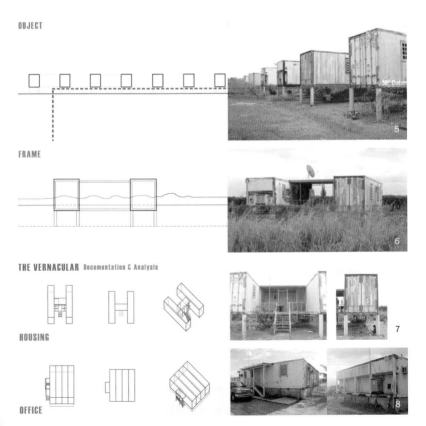

OBJECT

56" Datum

5

FRAME

6

THE VERNACULAR Documentation & Analysis

HOUSING

7

OFFICE

8

ANALYSIS 9: Work Shed_The typical work shed uses two containers joined by a wooden gabled roof. The connection of low-lying units creates shaded workspaces as well as storage areas on the ground. An axial tunnel effect occurs, visually framing the rich farm landscape. **10: Feed Storage_** The feed-storage building is created with eight containers connected side by side with a wooden canopy to mark the entrance. Joining multiple units laterally creates vast open interior space. The resulting volume negates the linear proportions of a single unit. The new exterior surface is a textured wall composed of abutting container doors. **11: Grain_**The meeting "room" within the four-container office structure is an example of space and light spanning across the linear grain of a single unit. Memory of the unit is retained at connections with typical deep wood soffits. **12: Inset_**The recessed door of the electrical shed forms an exterior porch. Setting back the enclosure wall creates a shaded space within the container proper; no additive construction is necessary. **13: Axis_**The eight-container storage shed creates a deep cross-grained interior. The party walls between adjacent containers are uniformly punctured with the remaining soffits serving as memories of the walls that were once there. The resultant space produces a strong axial spatiality whose transverse axes are amplified by natural light.

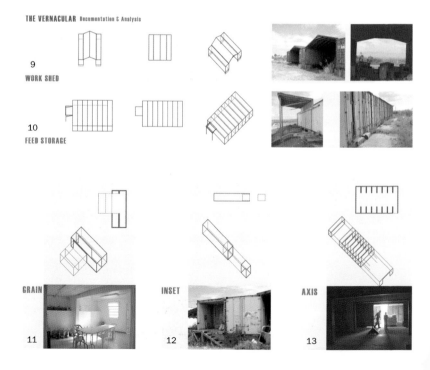

THE VERNACULAR Documentation & Analysis

9
WORK SHED

10
FEED STORAGE

GRAIN

INSET

AXIS

11

12

13

DESIGN **1**_scale of living **2**_model view from existing row of housing **3**_perceptual extensions
4_model view details

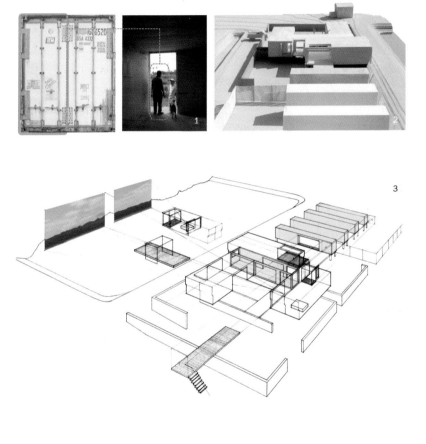

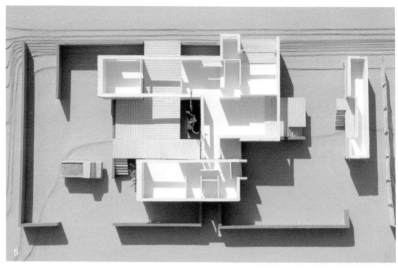

5

6

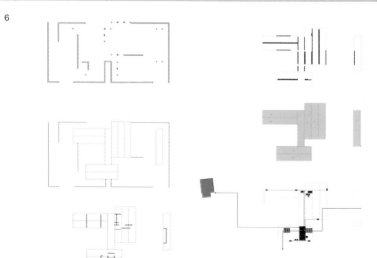

5_open model, aerial view **6**_construction operations **7**_below the fifty-six: infrastructural order beneath the datum **8**_container space: maximizing the given module

7

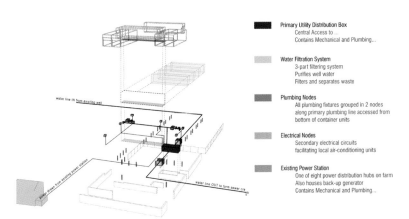

Primary Utility Distribution Box
Central Access to ...
Contains Mechanical and Plumbing...

Water Filtration System
3-part filtering system
Purifies well water
Filters and separates waste

Plumbing Nodes
All plumbing fixtures grouped in 2 nodes
along primary plumbing line accessed from
bottom of container units

Electrical Nodes
Secondary electrical circuits
facilitating local air-conditioning units

Existing Power Station
One of eight power distribution hubs on farm
Also houses back-up generator
Contains Mechanical and Plumbing...

8

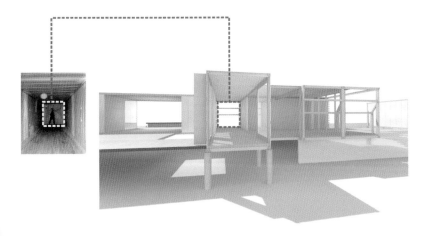

9_plan key: 1. car entry 2. entry 3. living room 4. kitchen/dining 5. guest bath 6. guest bedroom
7. deck/outdoor dining 8. office 9. master bedroom 10. master dressing room and bathroom
11. laundry room 12. sundeck 13. storage **10**_sectional elevations

9

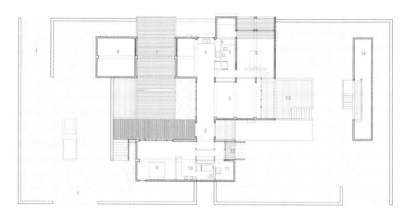

10

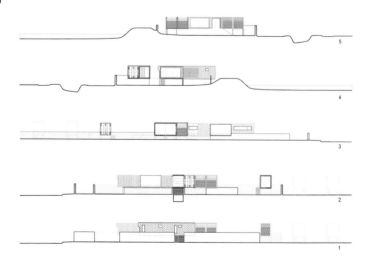

11_farmhouse exterior: view from northwest access road **12**_view from master bedroom to punch opening

Allston Loft

Dorchester, Massachusetts

The Allston Loft transformed the third level of a late-Victorian urban residence into a modern entertainment suite. Restoration of the first and second levels of the house was conducted by the owners, art collectors who wished to restore the house to its original decorative spirit. The top floor however, was to serve as a contemporary, minimalist diversion from the rest of the home.

The current space was a claustrophobic attic area with dropped ceilings and sequestered rooms and closets. After analyzing the existing roof structures, the space was gutted to reveal the geometrically intricate configurations of timber beams and roof surfaces. The primary objective was to expose the roof members and display them by means of an open gallerylike space, with modern furnishings, fixtures, and art. Materials such as stainless steel and frosted glass worked to contrast with the aging timbers that became the primary sculptural element within each space. The finished loft comprises a guest room, full bath, entertainment center, and bar.

The arrival landing and service areas are defined by low white ceilings, while the guest bedroom and the main loft space are restored to their maximum height. A low white wall and the original roof planks identify the guest bedroom and separate this private realm from the bar and entertainment area. Cracks between the original wood members are left to allow the penetration of light from the entertainment space to the sleeping space in order to engender a sense of lightness and spaciousness.

1

1_existing loft: photo of demolition process **2**_composite construction drawings

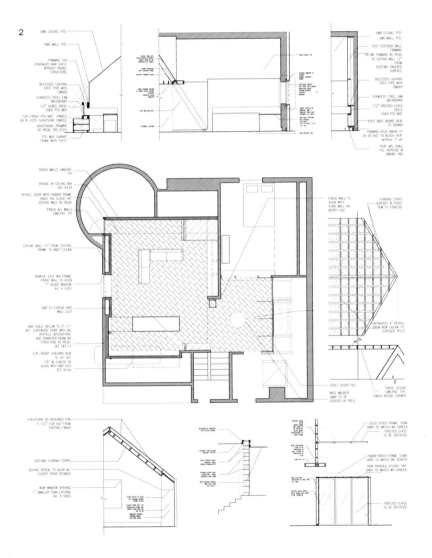

3

4

5

6

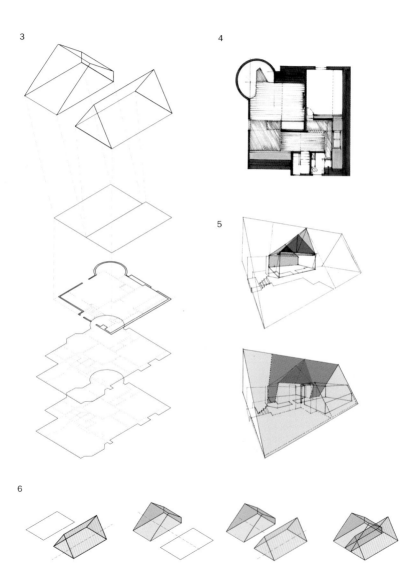

3_roof analysis **4**_schematic plan sketch **5/6**_roof analysis sketch **7**_view of entertainment space
8_sliding bar detail **9/10**_bar details **11**_entry foyer/stair landing **12**_view of bar

13_bar detail **14**_view from guest bedroom to entry foyer **15**_view from entry foyer to bathroom
16_guest bedroom **17**_view to stair framed by entry canopy

Schwartz Display Case

Schwartz Center for the Performing Arts / Cornell University /
Ithaca, New York

Overlooking Cayuga Gorge and serving as a popular venue for a community
theater, the Schwartz Center for the Performing Arts, a 1989 design by James
Stirling in Ithaca, New York, houses Cornell University's Department of Theater,
Film, and Dance. A 2001 design competition held by the Schwartz Center called
for entries focusing on the design and material characteristics of a display case
that could coexist with the existing lobby while elaborating on the center's
current activities.

The winning design by LOO was a minimal and practicable floating window-box,
a decidedly straighforward and modern response to Stirling's postmodern marble
expressiveness. The case appears to hover on the west wall of the lobby above
an existing wooden bench, combining with this existing object to emphasize clean
lines and shadows in an eclectically profiled lobby. In a simple compositional
gesture, a fifteen-foot wooden box slides out from a rectangular steel case,
producing an opening where brochures can be kept. The intersection of the two
volumes is faced with glass panels and serves as the display area. The stain-
less-steel box acts as a structural envelope from which the warmer wooden box
emerges to visually associate with the bench below. The surface of the metal is
adorned with lettering composed so as to dedicate the project in the same
slipping-and-sliding manner as the case itself.

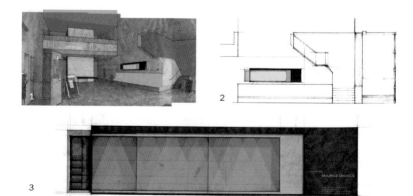

1

2

3

1_lobby photo collage
2_elevation sketch
3_display-case elevation
4_sliding wood-box drawing
5_axon of sliding boxes
6_viewing case
7_view of lobby with display case
8_view of display case as installed
above existing bench
9_material detail: wood, glass,
steel

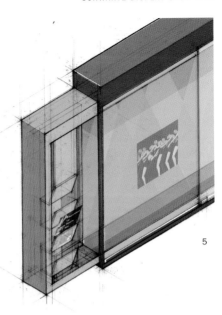

Borough Market
Tower Bridge / London, England

Submitted to Southwark City Council in 2005, this proposal for an extension to Borough Market on London's Southbank engages a practical formal response to the palimpsest of legislative and constructional restraints that have been imposed on a compact and complex site. By engaging the existing archeological, legislative, and constructive pressures of the site without a preconceived hierarchy, the proposal blankets the land proposed for regeneration with a conceptual grid that both registers the intricate palimpsest of existing conditions and defines the formal language of the market's extension.

The site, home to an active two-thousand-year-old food market, straddles both ancient Roman ruins and the remains of the fourteenth-century Winchester Palace while housing various late-nineteenth- and early-twentieth-century warehouses. By identifying and then isolating only the essential, delaminated elements of these protected, preserved remains, the overlaid grid defines the zones of permissible engagement. The conceptual blanket begins as a strict Cartesian grid that is subsequently distorted and skewed by both buried and visible physical constraints.

While the subterranean Roman and Gothic remains intermittently preclude the imposition of structural foundations across large zones of the site, one warehouse contains a listed interior timber frame while another provides a concrete structural skeleton for future appropriation. Nested within a dense network of medieval streets, the proposal introduces a market extension and community culinary program that becomes perceptibly distorted by these buried and visible physical restraints.

The aforementioned conceptual blanket acts as an indexical device to negotiate these constraints and is, in turn, materialized as a distorted and folded concrete shell that is formally responsive to the legal and tangible realities of the existing condition. By delaminating the existing exterior surface of one warehouse from its concrete skeleton and preserving the protected timbers of the other, the conceptual blanket both respects and physically delineates the complexities of the contorted site. Urbanistically, the solution provides a public pedestrian pathway system with ubiquitous social and economic infrastructures.

1_market site plan and unfolded elevations **2**_analysis diagrams: site constraints and "blanket" activation

1

2

3_site program and strategy diagrams **4**_generation and distortion of modulating grid
5_taxonomy of formal manipulations

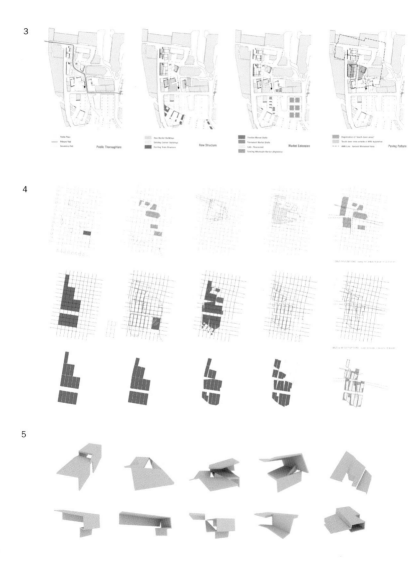

6_concrete-frame integration diagrams **7**_timber-frame conservation diagrams
8_archeological palimpsest: Roman and Gothic remains to be preserved **9**_warehouse: existing
concrete frame structure **10**_existing warehouse: listed timber frame to be conserved and exposed

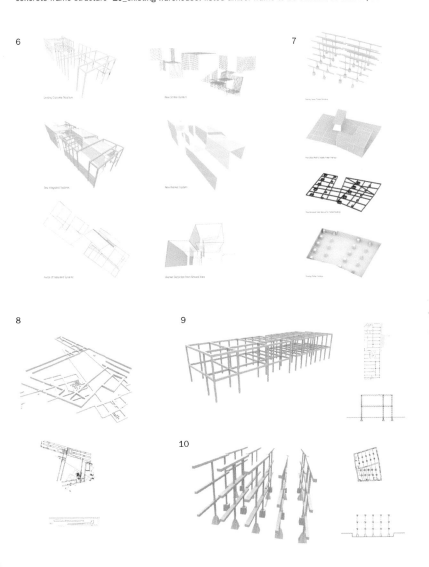

11

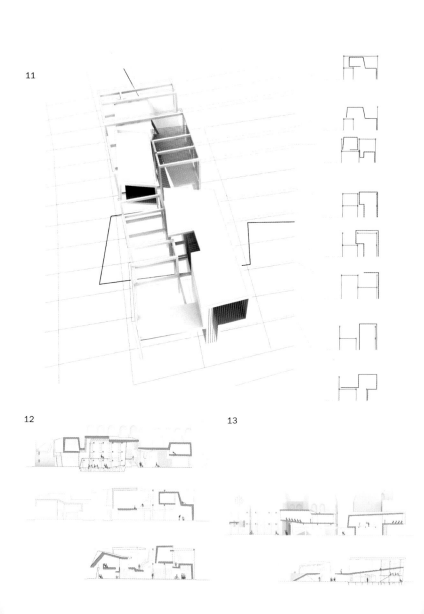

12

13

11_appropriated concrete frame **12**_transverse sections: market and restaurant
13_longitudinal section: culinary programs **14**_encased timber frame **15**_view of elevated terrace
16_market expansion from south

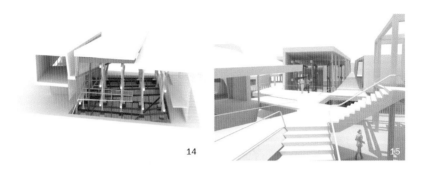

14

15

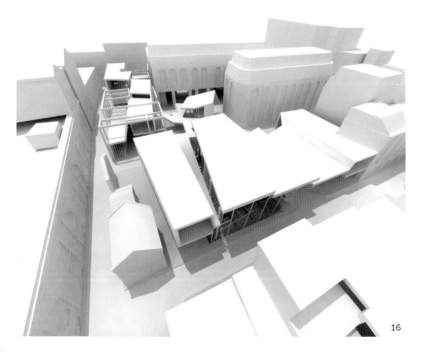

16

Interboro

INSIDE THE OLIGOPTICON

We've become experts in entropy. Or so it would seem. Recently, we won two competitions: one about a "dead mall," and one about a "shrinking city." We should be terribly cynical by now.

But somehow, we've never been more hopeful.

We're not sure, but we think it has something to do with the way we situate ourselves. When we looked closely at our sites, we felt a pulse where others had felt none. While others weaved narratives of sickness and death out of abandoned storefronts, overgrown parking lots, and weathered murals, we learned— by hanging out, talking to people, and watching what was going on—that the very same phenomena can be conditions for new and exciting kinds of life.

These are the sorts of things you learn when you situate yourself on the ground. You learn that there are winners and losers even in death. You learn how to empathize with an enormous variety of frameworks, logics, and disciplines. You learn how to situate yourself in many (often contradictory) roles.

If architects and planners sometimes strive for a totalizing, comprehensive view, we strive to embrace the seeming infinity of conflicting, partial views. We've abandoned the panoptic for the "oligoptic," to borrow a word from Bruno Latour. In the following pages, we've organized our work along three paths, three roles, three types of situations relevant to an oligoptic approach to planning.

1. DETECTIVE WORK

Keep to the actors! Because there are tens of thousands of things you could never deduce from conventional narratives about, for example, dead malls and shrinking cities. This is why it's important to do good detective work: old-fashioned empirical observation. The problem with architects and planners isn't so much that they always think they have the answer, it's that they always think they know the problem. We have to listen more and talk less. You know, like detectives do.

2. GHOSTWRITING

The people and the places you'll encounter in the three projects presented here are like celebrities: they're too busy doing their thing to stop to document how important their thing is. That's where ghostwriters come in. Ghostwriters create legacies, lobbying for their subject's importance by telling a story about how integral the subject is to the development of the world.

Similarly, in all of the places we've worked in, we've identified people on the ground whose self-interested actions are clues about how to make the place better. What these people need is someone to "sing their life," so to speak, to legitimize these self-interested practices and make the case that they are vital to a place's future.

3. THE LIFE COACH

The third phase is the toughest phase because unlike detective work—which is about observation and documentation—and ghostwriting—which is about interpretation—life coaching entails advocating for a person or a place. More ambitiously, it entails advocating for a particular outcome. What's going to happen to the Dutchess Mall? Who knows, but if you're a good life coach, you can map many possible futures, pick one that you think is the most interesting, equitable, sustainable, or maybe just feasible, and "rig" the game so that it plays out in your favor. Is this cheating? Maybe, but that's what we're hired for.

In the Meantime, Life with Landbanking
Fishkill, New York

In the Meantime, Life with Landbanking is our winning entry to the Los Angeles Forum for Architecture and Urban Design's Dead Malls competition, which asked entrants to envision a future for a dead shopping mall of the entrant's choosing.

On the third day of a whirlwind tour of the suburbs of New York City, we came across our subject: the Dutchess Mall in Fishkill, New York. A classic regional shopping mall built in 1974, it had been build at a then seemingly perfect location: the southeast corner of a major highway interchange in the heart of a county poised for growth. But the market nuances at an individual site can be hard to predict; it turned out that this site was all wrong for a shopping center. The region around it has grown steadily over the past three decades, but Poughkeepsie to the north was the magnet for that growth. Even as the Dutchess Mall was dying, a vital suburban strip evolved on the ten-mile stretch just north of the interstate. By the early 1990s, it was less than 50 percent occupied, and in 1998, it officially closed its doors.

But it didn't die. Detective work revealed that the Dutchess Mall is playing host organism to scores of different bacterial cultures that infuse the site with life. You don't need a microscope to see these new growths on the weekends when the popular Dutchess Flea Market fills up the old Service Merchandise anchor store and parking lot with crafts, antiques, hardware, hair salons, specialty foods, heavy-metal memorabilia, and lots and lots of junk. Lots of other activities—formal and informal, scheduled and erratic, sanctioned and illicit—happen on the site too: driver's license testing and practice, roving food carts, prostitutes meeting clients, truck and mobile-home storage, carpool meetings, and even the occasional motorcycle rally, political protest, or UFO sighting.

Let's not overstate the case: decay is ominous. The point is that beyond it (and this is something planners often don't get beyond) there is a pulse: faint signals here and there, a breath, a murmur, a blip on the EKG that we should, like good doctors, be aware of. Far from having died, the mall has merely transformed.

In the Meantime, Life With Landbanking stems from our suspicion that there is a logic to these faint signals, and that we might do well to emulate that logic. In the spirit of endogenous development—or development that identifies and takes inspiration from the urbanity that exists in a given place, however trivial it might seem—our programs are ones that can be imagined being developed out of cultures that have already started to grow around the property. The result is not a master plan but a collection of small, cheap, feasible moves that can come in over time and lead to many possible futures.

It may be the case that with time, a cure will be found, and Dutchess Mall will make a full recovery, probably reborn as a distribution, manufacturing, or research center. It's certainly what the developers—who freely admit to land-banking the property—are hoping for. We are not against the future possibility of such an invasive operation. But in the meantime, we wonder if there aren't options for some alternative therapies...

These alternative therapies fall into two categories: short-term projects that will make good use of the site during the landbanking phase and more perma-nent (though still very flexible) projects that can help prepare it to be strategically redeveloped at a future date.

1. CLINICAL TRIAL: INCUBATE HEALING CULTURES

Hotbox, Nightclub, Beer Garden, Summer Stage, Sculpture Garden, Car Wash, Recycling Center | The first set of interventions consists of short-term experi-mental trials to complement existing site dynamics and plant seeds for new ones. There is already a rich network of marginal users taking advantage of the site in informal ways. The new programs we suggest can vivify and make further use of the space but, like the flea market, are not so spatially rooted that they cannot be displaced one day for a more profitable land use.

2. GENE THERAPY: ALTER THE CODE

Daycare Center, Recreation Commons, Bus Stop, Monument | Another set of projects is about inscribing new program elements into the DNA of the site. No matter what its future, these long-term preventative measures can help fight future disease and decay. They add value, potentially making the site more attractive to future investors and tenants of all kinds, and can hybridize with existing and new programs. Their forms are cheap and flexible: ultimately disposable but also easy to upgrade in hopes that they may permanently take root.

1_a dog from the start: views of the Dutchess Mall in Fishkill, New York

1

2_Lou and his pickle stand have become community fixtures at the weekend flea market.
3_Fishkill Cleaners is the last legitimate business left in the mall. **4**_Larry is the manager for
the hundreds of vendors who now occupy the former department store.

5_medical diagrams monitor the mall's health **6**_While most of the life has drained out of the inside of the mall, a few vestigial programs remain, and new, opportunistic ones have flourished around its edges.

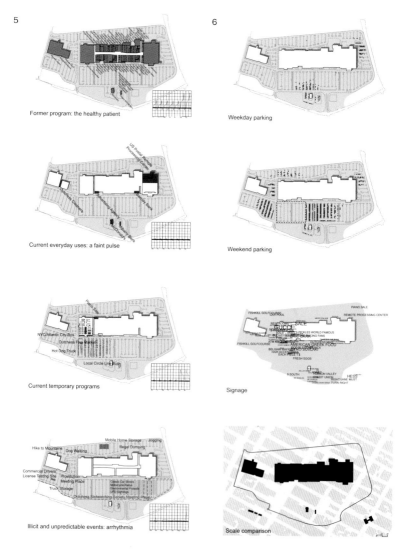

5

Former program: the healthy patient

Current everyday uses: a faint pulse

Current temporary programs

Illicit and unpredictable events: arrhythmia

6

Weekday parking

Weekend parking

Signage

Scale comparison

7_existing site **8**_Lots of little moves might eventually add up to a wholly transformed space: a new life built from the outside in from what's already there.

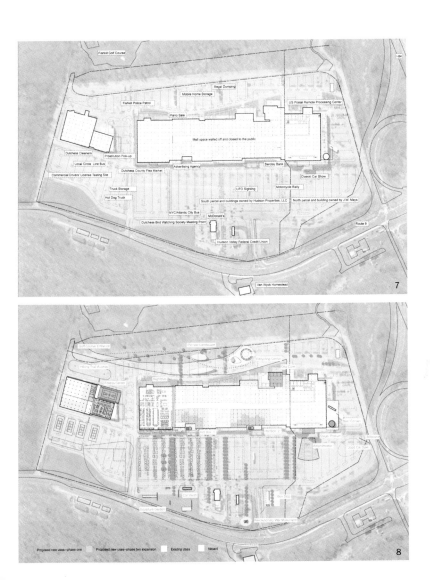

9_The outside wall of the building is replaced with a more permeable facade, turning the mall inside out. **10**_The mall stores used to front in the internal corridor, with a service yard in the back. **11**_A "hotbox" creates a new entry from the outside while providing shared office infrastructure for small businesses.

9

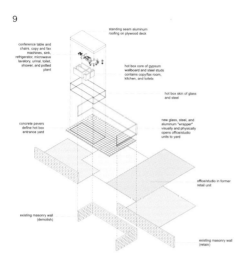

10

11

12_view of the existing service area **13**_The hotboxes are freestanding structures in the service yards with conference room/lounge, washroom, and basic office equipment. **14**_A sculpture garden fills in the gaps around a new car wash and existing ATM and McDonald's—a radically mixed-use drive-thru zone for art and everyday errands. **15**_The strip center outparcel is economically remodeled as a fitness center. **16**_Plugging a fitness bubble into the rear service yard allows for a cheap temporary gymnasium; the existing retail space becomes the lockers and gym.

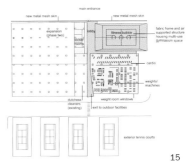

17_ Though flexible and temporary, our proposals leave their mark no matter what the developers ultimately decide to do. A few possible futures are imagined from their germination (second row from top) to their incubation (third row from top) and through to their metastasis (bottom row), which could be many things—office park, residential community, a park, maybe even a new mall. Or perhaps a heterotopic hybrid, something yet to be imagined.

17

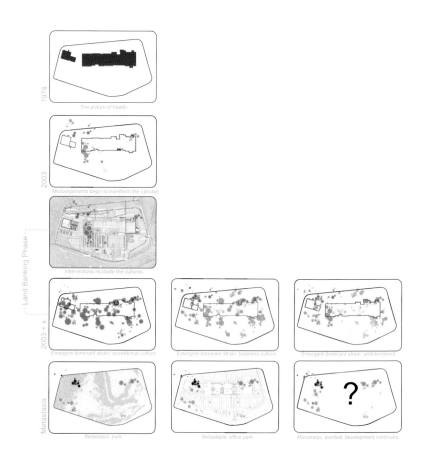

18_In the meantime, life with landbanking...

18

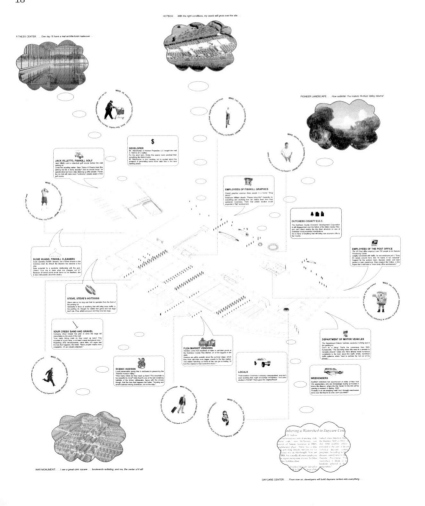

Reutan Sands
Chicago, Illinois

Not to diss Daniel Burnham or anything, but it's important to remember that he wasn't the only Chicago planner worthy of such a time-honored legacy. On July 10, 1886, a former Mississippi River boat captain and circus owner named George Wellington "Cap" Streeter set sail from downtown Chicago on his ship, the *Reutan*, and promptly got marooned a few hundred feet off the coast. After several days, the natural currents of the lake started blowing sand and silt up against the boat, creating a small island. Cap, entrepreneur that he was, opened a trading post right there on the spot. He named the new land "Streeterville" and immediately declared himself governor.

In subsequent years, Streeterville grew to encompass hundreds of acres, which Cap controlled for nearly thirty years until the city finally forced him out. In that time, Streeterville became something of a heterotopia, a haven for the illicit activities the city proper wouldn't tolerate. Cap, not surprisingly, was reluctant to see it go. Though the city prevailed, Cap's legacy lives on, as much of downtown Chicago sits on the *Reutan*'s sands.

Reutan Sands is a recommended submission to the Graham Foundation's 21st-Century Lakefront Park Competition, which asked entrants to envision a park on the northern-most two miles of Chicago lakefront. It is Interboro's tribute to Cap, a self-interested, informal actor who managed to have as big an impact on Chicago's future as Daniel Burnham.

Reutan Sands begins with a simple observation: Chicago's existing lakefront is organized in north-south bands of city, park, then water. In each band, one moves freely north and south, but moving east and west is more difficult, more of an "event." The bands rarely overlap.

Inspired by Cap, we proposed new public spaces to work as "stitches" that traverse lake and city as a new kind of in-between, weaving the park more palpably into everyday life and creating hybrid spaces between the busy rhythms of the city and the natural expanse of the lake. The new park is not a buffer or a grand reprieve, but a third space that emerges when city and lake meet face to face.

Our vision involves four organizational principles:

1. STREETS
The city streets push out to the east, bringing the specific qualities of each neighborhood into contact with the water's edge.

2. INCREMENTAL LAND FILL
Over time, the lake's natural processes (littoral drift) will fill in the spaces between each street extension with new land, supplemented with fill as needed.

3. PATH
By creating new land, we make space to introduce a public walk/bike path, extending Chicago's system of continuous public waterfront access from Lincoln Park north to the city's northern limit.

4. DEVELOPMENT
The infrastructural stitches between city and lake will bring the benefits of lakefront public amenities deeper into each neighborhood. Over time, new, more diverse programs associated with lakefront programming will spark up near each stitch.

These are not fixed strategies; they are a set of flexible interventions that can be phased. The resulting variety of conditions can serve immediate needs, provide an interesting interim landscape, and ultimately have a transformative impact on the neighborhood. It is a process of additive chance that does not seek to radically disrupt but allows new typologies to emerge when existing spatial qualities are expressed in a new context.

1_four-part strategy: streets, landfill, path, and development
2_The flexible and nonhierarchical plan allows the park to evolve incrementally, in harmony with local community needs, the changing development market, and the natural processes of the lake.

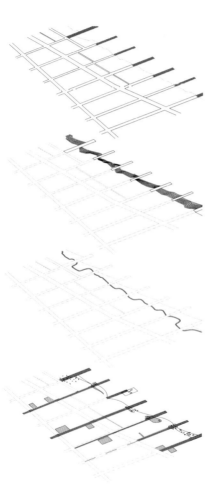

1

2

3_The existing lakefront is discontinuous; where it can be accessed, it is used in an everyday, backyard kind of way.

4_This pier, or "stitch," connects the lakefront to the city with much-needed recreational uses—a protected swimming area in the lake, with a seasonal ice/roller-skating folly in the park.

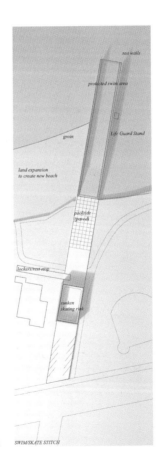

3

4 *SWIM/SKATE STITCH*

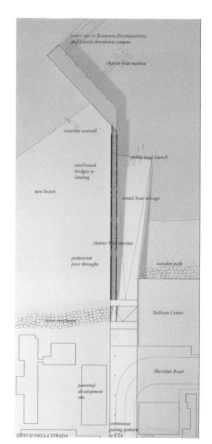

water taxi to Evanston (Northwestern)
and Loyola downtown campus

charter boat marina

concrete seawall

public boat launch

steel/wood
bridges to
landing

new beach

rental boat storage

charter boat marina

pedestrian
pass throughs

wooden path

Loyola CTA
platform
extension

Sullivan Center

stone revetment

Sheridan Road

Loyola Park

potential
development
site

continuous
paving pattern
to CTA

STITCH DELLA STRADA

5

5_At the Loyola campus, the north-south axis is interrupted with a multimodal pier linking the inland transit facilities to new forms of water transport. **6**_In this dense neighborhood, we propose a major recreation pier with a screen and seating area, suitable for sporting events by day and film festivals by night.

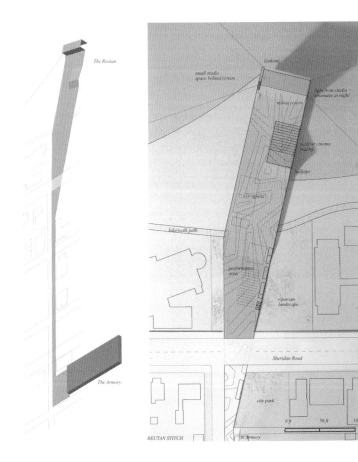

The Reutan

lookout

*small studio
space behind screen*

*light from studio
emanates at night*

movie screen

*outdoor cinema
seating*

halfpipe

sports

bike/walk path

*performance
area*

*riparian
landscape*

Sheridan Road

The Armory

city park

0 ft   50 ft   100 ft

REUTAN STITCH   *to Armory*

However Unspectacular
Detroit, Michigan

There's a story people love to tell about Detroit. Beginning with the invention of the assembly line, it traces Detroit's rise to Fordist paradise, notes the city's role in the making of the modern middle class, and then waxes poetic about some urban version of the American Dream that a combination of industrial restructuring, antiurban federal policies, and racism brought to an untimely end. The story's next chapter is about Detroit's decline: it takes us through deindustrialization, race riots, and the suburban exodus and ends by speculating that Detroit is a city that has "outlived itself." In a postscript, the story's author, who is now walking around "the ruins of Detroit," points to the trees that are growing through streets and factory floors, the houses that have crumbled into the earth, the deer population that has colonized downtown, and concludes that one day, Detroit will revert to nature.

Some people who tell this story are thrilled by this prospect. So much so that they come up with ways to facilitate it. James Corner, for example, has proposed roping it off. Camilo Vergara has proposed turning the city into a museum of ruins.

However sexy this story is, we'd like to offer another reading. We agree that Detroit will gradually be reclaimed by its environment, but we don't take this to mean that in, say, fifty years Detroit will look like a prairie. That's because if left to its own accord, Detroit will not revert to "nature." Left to its own accord, Detroit will revert to the suburbs. Today it's the suburbs, not the indigenous landscape, that you can count on to fill in whatever hole civilization has created. It's the most ravenous, opportunistic force around.

There's no lack of evidence of this in Detroit. When Mayor Kwame Kilpatrick recently took developers on a tour of new buildings in Detroit, most of his exhibits looked like buildings you'd expect to find outside the city. The fact is that much of Detroit's new development is happening at lower densities.

Would the continued suburbanization of Detroit be a bad thing?

Potentially. If it followed the national trend, the outlook is bleak. Whites would repopulate the city, Blacks would be relocated to inner-ring suburbs, and a period of exacerbated racial tension and pious handwringing over gentrification would precede the final outcome: a White low-density city, rich in services and opportunities and surrounded by an impoverished ring of Black suburbs.

However Unspectacular is Interboro's winning entry to the German Federal Cultural Foundation's Shrinking Cities competition. A collaboration with the Center for Urban Pedagogy (CUP), the project stems from our conviction that the suburbanization of Detroit doesn't have to follow national trends. In the context of an analysis of various "modes" of Detroit suburbanization, we identified the seeds of a "New Suburbanism" that we think could potentially "even things out," or make Detroit less of an anomaly (less of a spectacle) in a metropolitan region marked by robust growth.

What is the New Suburbanism? The process—one of "bottom-up" suburbanization—happens when vacant lots, having been abandoned by their owners, are taken, borrowed, or bought by neighboring entrepreneurial landowners. What results—a de-densification but also a "replatting" that undermines official property boundaries—is the New Suburbanism.

How can we help this process along? Instead of emphasizing the sexy new developments that are helping to gentrify Detroit's and many other American cities' downtowns, we take the small-scale efforts already underway by individual residents or small groups to improve their lot and increase their space as our inspiration. Our proposal is a collection of modest initiatives that build upon common-sense ideas pioneered by community-development groups across the country. In each instance, the hope is that the initiatives will make the New Suburbanism more vital, more equitable, and more feasible.

We are not setting out to radically transform Detroit into a revamped version of the middle-class utopia it once was, nor a hip playground for a well-educated urban elite. Elements of both of these visions will come once there are more opportunities to improve individual circumstances and properties. Our ideas help widen the range of opportunities. Although they could lead to many possible futures, the simple result we hope for is that residents and businesses get more space and increase their property values. Detroit's vacant lots—so prevalent and so stigmatized throughout the city—become valuable assets, as they would be if we found them in the suburbs.

1_As ghostwriters, we realized that we were witnessing suburbanization from the bottom-up. By taking over adjacent yards and "improving their lot," people are altering the genetic code of the city.

1

2_few existing examples of how parts of Detroit's grid have become more suburban with new building types and lower densities

2

Victoria Park, snipped from the grid and protected by a green belt

Victoria Park, before suburbanization

Victoria Park, after suburbanization

Open space as a security measure

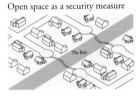

The Belt

1940
6.7 dwelling units
per acre

1992
3.56 dwelling units
per acre

-47% decrease in residential density, from 1940 to 1992

Lafayette Park, towers and townhouses framing a 17 acre park

Lafayette Park, a.k.a. "Black Bottom," before suburbanization

Lafayette Park, after suburbanization

Open space as recreational amenity

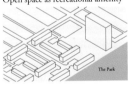

The Park

1940
6.7 dwelling units
per acre

1960
2.97 dwelling units
per acre

-66% decrease in residential density, from 1940 to 1960

Elmhurst, where residents increase their lot size and open space amenity by purchasing adjacent vacant lots

Elmhurst, before suburbanization

Elmhurst, after suburbanization

Open space as personal equity

The Parcel

1953
40.0 dwelling units
per acre

2004
5.2 dwelling units
per acre

-87% decrease in residential density, from 1953 to 2004

3_We began with the true story of Wanda Cowans and Helen McMurray, two sisters whose entrepreneurialism provides a perfect introduction to the New Suburbanism. **4**_Because of abandonment and depressed values on their block, they were able to buy two homes plus the intermediary vacant lot. **5**_The result of Wanda and Helen's efforts is a new typology of sorts: the lot for two sisters!

3

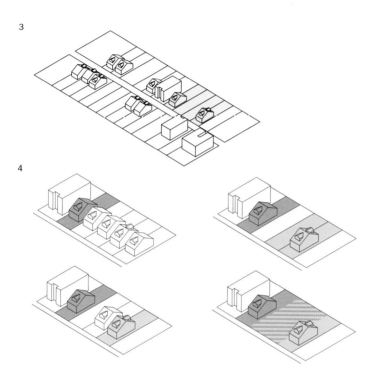

4

5

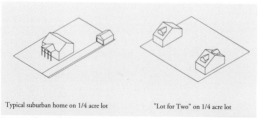

Typical suburban home on 1/4 acre lot   "Lot for Two" on 1/4 acre lot

Emergence of a new suburban type

6_The story of the block is also the story of the city: in the 1950s and 1960s, the city grew to be a solid collection of middle-class, auto-oriented neighborhoods. **7/8**_With the decline of the auto industry and the riots of the 1960s, Detroit suffered a massive out-migration to the suburbs; many properties were abandoned and eventually demolished or burnt down (vacant lots shown in blue). **9**_This abandonment and disinvestment continued until recent times. We suggest a collection of modest initiatives that build upon common-sense ideas pioneered by community-development groups across the country to help residents reinvent their neighborhoods at lower densities. **10/11**_With a little help, Wanda and Helen could improve their "lot" and set a precedent in their community.

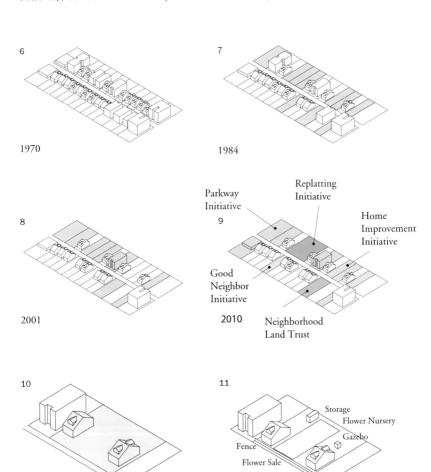

6

1970

7

1984

8

2001

9

Parkway Initiative

Replatting Initiative

Home Improvement Initiative

Good Neighbor Initiative

2010

Neighborhood Land Trust

10

11

Storage
Flower Nursery
Gazebo
Fence
Flower Sale

What is today a purely reactive policy could be utilized to create opportunity. We propose that the city become more proactive in replatting the land, providing a mix of parcels in different shapes and sizes that could accommodate suburban programs and inscribe a degree of long-term heterogeneity. **12**_Scenario I: The School expands into the adjacent replatted parcels. **13**_Scenario II: The replatted parcels are developed with suburban housing types.

12

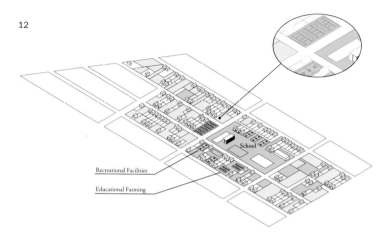

Recreational Facilities

Educational Farming

School

13

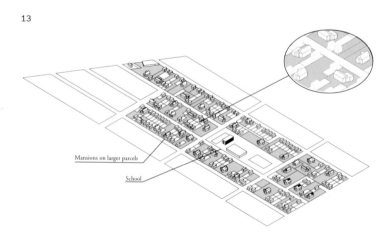

Mansions on larger parcels

School

14_Scenario III: Replatting for diverse parcel sizes and shapes allows for the development of various suburban and urban programs. **15**_Pessimistic Scenario: Of course, it's possible that nothing would happen...

14

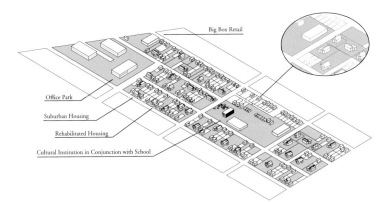

15

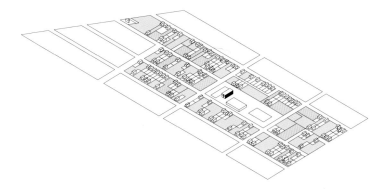